OCR

D1358726

In Charge of Customer Satisfaction

In Charge
Series Editor: Roger Cartwright

Managing People
Roger Cartwright, Michael Collins, George Green and Anita Candy

Managing Operations
Roger Cartwright, Michael Collins, George Green and Anita Candy

Managing Finance and Information
Roger Cartwright, Michael Collins, George Green and Anita Candy

In Charge of Yourself
Roger Cartwright, Michael Collins, George Green and Anita Candy

In Charge of Customer Satisfaction
Roger Cartwright and George Green

In Charge of Customer Satisfaction

Roger Cartwright • George Green

BLACKWELL
Business

First published 1997

First published in USA 1997

2 4 6 8 10 9 7 5 3 1

Blackwell Publishers Ltd
108 Cowley Road
Oxford OX4 1JF
UK

Blackwell Publishers Inc
238 Main Street
Cambridge, Massachusetts 02142,
USA

British Library Cataloguing in Publication Data

A CIP catalogue record for this book is available from the British Library.

Library of Congress Cataloging-in-Publication Data

Cartwright, Roger.
    In charge of customer satisfaction : a competence approach / Roger Cartwright and George Green.
        p.   cm. – (In charge)
    Includes bibliographical references and index.
    ISBN 0–631–20087–9 (alk. paper)
        1. Consumer satisfaction.   I. Green, George.   II. Title.
    III. Series.
    HF5415.335.C37   1997   96–23266
    658.8'12–dc20   CIP
ISBN 0–631–200878

Phototypeset in 11.5 on 14pt Palatino
by Intype London Ltd
Printed in Great Britain by T.J. Press (Padstow) Ltd., Padstow, Cornwall

This book is printed on acid-free paper

Contents

List of Figures

Preface

'Customer Satisfaction is: customer needs and expectations being met all of the time, every time throughout the life of the product or service. Without this you have no customer loyalty.' (N. Jones, Premier Exhausts, Unipart Group of Companies)

It was John Wanamaker, the owner of a Philadelphia department store in the 1860s, who coined the phrase, 'The customer is always right', but by the 1920s Henry Ford only offered customers for his Model T car, 'Any colour you like as long as it's black'. In the 1990s the customer is king or queen: if choosing a car, there is a wide range of models, options, engines and colours. As competition has increased, so the needs of the customer are becoming paramount. As Naresh Goyal, chairman of Jet Airways in India, has written, 'Any airline may get you from place to place, but what happens between take off and landing is what makes the difference'. New expressions have entered organizational language:

- 'Customer care'
- 'Customer recovery'
- 'Decision making at the point of delivery'
- 'Customer led not product driven'
- 'Total quality systems'
- 'Marketing mix'
- 'Market segmentation'
- 'Repeat business'
- 'Value chains'
- 'Internal customers and markets'

and many others.

A few blocks up from the bookshop of Bill Shepard (whom we will meet in chapter 3) in the UK market town of Bicester is the Yin Hong Chinese restaurant run by Andy Ng (not to be confused with the Mr Ng of Raffles considered in chapter 3; Ng is a common

Far Eastern surname). The Yin Hong is in the centre of a town that is one of the fastest growing in the UK, due to its proximity to the M40 motorway from London to Birmingham, and which possesses a number of satellite communities, nearly all of which have a Chinese takeaway fast food establishment. What is interesting is that people from these communities will drive into the centre of town, park their vehicles and obtain their takeaway meals from the restaurant. Bicester is not renowned for its nightlife, although it was the major town serving the now closed USAF base at Upper Heyford and one of the British Army's major logistics depots (COD Bicester), and thus it is not easy to attract evening custom. The quality of the food and the excellent, welcoming service is such that people will drive past three or four competitor establishments in order to obtain their food at the Yin Hong and then drive home again to eat it. One can understand people driving to eat in the restaurant but for people to drive out, collect a takeaway and then drive home past a number of other establishments offering the same basic service suggests that Andy Ng and his staff are 'doing something right'. They are not cheaper than the other establishments but the food is of high quality and the service is excellent.

The Yin Hong is mentioned because it exemplifies the major concept in customer satisfaction; it is *convincing the customer to drive past the competition to purchase your product or service*. That is what this book is all about. The organizations mentioned have all managed this task; because they go the extra (metaphorical) mile for their customers, the customers will go an extra (metaphorical) mile to acquire the product or service. In the case of the Yin Hong, they are real extra miles.

Today's successful organizations realize that the customer has a choice. As part of a two-year programme for all staff worldwide, Robert Ayling, speaking as the then Group Managing Director of British Airways, stated that, 'It costs five times as much to win a new customer as to retain an old one', a lesson all organizations and those working within them should take to heart.

The days of customer relations belonging only to a customer service or a complaints department are on the wane. Current good practice dictates that, firstly, everybody in an organization has a customer, whether that customer be internal or external, and, secondly, that all those in the organization have a duty to the final, end user customer. That means that all staff, from the most junior to the most senior, need an appreciation of what products or services the organization offers and, secondly, an understanding of the wants and needs of both their personal and the ultimate customer. In short, we all have customers and, in the long term, only good service will retain these customers.

This book will be useful not only for those in the UK and the USA but also for those in the rest of the world. The volume uses examples from both sides of the Atlantic and from Asia.

Customer care and customer service ideas began, not surprisingly, in the retail sector but, as this book will show you, they are now equally applicable in manufacturing and service industries as well as in retail, and also to those working in the public sector, schools, local authorities, the civil service/Federal Government as well as the voluntary sector. The customer may be known as a 'client' or a 'recipient' but he or she is still a customer. Within the pages of this book, you will meet real people who work and provide excellent customer service in a variety of organizations, both large and small, including shops, airlines, the healthcare sector, government, leisure and railways. This book will show you how they make the crucial difference.

In 1994, a set of standards to support National Vocational Qualification Level 3 (NVQ3) in customer service was published in the UK, and this book supports those using these standards as a vehicle to examine the concepts of customer care they need to assist them in the workplace.

You may be in a supervisory or a junior management position; you may be seeking such a role; or you may just have an interest in customer service – whatever your circumstances, this book will assist you in your relationships with your and your organization's customers, and, indeed, in your role as a customer yourself.

The Standards were drawn up by the Customer Services Lead Body sponsored by the Department of Employment in the UK. Following normal N/SVQ practice, the Standards consist of Units of Competence which are divided into related Elements of Competence. The full Standards also divide Elements into associated Performance Criteria against which assessment is made in the case of formal qualifications; Range Statements, which define the range of situations and contexts within which competence needs to be developed; and finally the requisite Knowledge and Understanding that is necessary for the effective demonstration of competence.

In common with other volumes in the *In Charge* series, this book takes a holistic approach and does not seek to look at the standards in detail, but it is important to know that Customer Service has become so vital that competence standards have been developed to reflect good practice. The authorship team's experience with competence-based approaches have shown that this holistic approach is an effective way forward, as it encourages the reader to look at the total picture rather than at small items in isolation. This book concerns itself with the Knowledge and Understanding necessary to demonstrate competence in customer service. Those undertaking qualifications based on the Standards will have full details of them as part of their programme materials.

While this book contains all the relevant knowledge and understanding you will require to understand customer service and satisfaction, it also presents real examples for you to consider. The authors have observed and interviewed a number of people in the UK and other parts of Europe, the Middle East, India and the USA – people in jobs like yours, people who sell, who care for others, who provide a service – and it is their experiences that are used to bring the concepts to life. It is no coincidence that all of those interviewed and studied work for successful organizations, which can be defined as those that practice customer service and care. You will meet them and their customers through the pages of this book and you will be able to use their experiences to improve your own customer relationships. Because the examples span the world and a variety of work sectors, it is possible to examine the effects of differing cultural attitudes to service, thus this book seeks to meet the needs of those involved in the delivery of customer service, wherever they may live and work. Within this volume you will find examples from retail outlets and the travel industry, where people are meeting the customer face to face, through to industrial situations where the customer might never meet the personnel of an organization but where customer service is just as important.

Considerable care has been taken to research situations and interview those involved in the delivery of high quality customer care. A number of cases are taken from the travel industry because, first, this is a sector that is at the sharp end of customer satisfaction, which provides very comprehensive examples that you can then relate to your own organization, and secondly because customer interactions within this sector are possibly the closest one can get to those in a 'closed system'. The concepts of closed and open systems are part of General Systems Theory, which has its roots in biological science. A closed system is one that would be totally sealed and would have no interaction with the external environment. No such systems occur in nature – our cells and organs must take nutrients and air in from the outside environment and must also remove wastes to the outside – but the concept is useful in that if we can remove extraneous factors in a customer interaction, we may be able to see more clearly what is actually happening. To this end, we could consider a cruise liner or a long-haul airline flight as being a relatively closed system in which we can observe the behaviour of suppliers and customers in a more focused manner.

The book is laid out as follows:

Chapter 1: Knock, Knock, Who's There? Who is the customer? The customer's wants and needs
Chapter 2: Getting to Know You. Understanding your market
Chapter 3: Great Expectations. Getting it right the first time
Chapter 4: Where Everybody Knows Your Name. Effective communication
Chapter 5: I Don't Like to Complain, but . . . . Complaints, feedback and recovery
Chapter 6: Help, I Need Somebody; Help. Problem solving
Chapter 7: The Times They Are A-Changin'. The management and ownership of change
Chapter 8: I Can't Get No Satisfaction. A whole 'pack' of howlers

The book will also introduce you to the Ten Golden Rules of Customer Care:

1 **It costs far more to gain a new customer than to retain an existing one.**
2 **Unless you recover the situation quickly, a lost customer will be lost forever.**
3 **Dissatisfied customers have far more friends than satisfied ones.**
4 **The customer is not always right, but how you tell them that they're wrong can make all the difference and ultimately they do pay your wages.**

5 Welcome complaints; they allow for recovery.
6 In a free market economy, never forget that the customer has a choice.
7 Treat internal customers as you would external ones.
8 You must listen to your customers to find out what they want.
9 If you don't believe, how can you expect the customer to?
10 If you don't look after your customers, somebody else will.

These themes will be elaborated through the experiences of the people you will meet in the various chapters and the philosophies of their senior managers and employing organizations.

HOW TO USE THIS BOOK

No book, however well written, can provide the answer to a specific problem that an individual has encountered. However, by providing the individual with an insight into the processes that are at work within situations and with opportunities to examine situations from a variety of standpoints, books such as those in the *In Charge* series can allow you to make more informed decisions.

How individuals use these books will depend on the situations they find themselves in. It might be that:

1 You are taking a customer service course and have been advised to read chapter 4 to support your classroom work. In that case, you should consider the material in the light of the lectures and seminars you have attended and use the information in the book to support the taught input.
2 You may be involved in an open learning programme, in which case the book can add to the information contained in your open learning programme.
3 If you are attending a company-based short course, this book will provide you with extra information and can be used to explore areas that you have developed a special interest in.
4 Perhaps you have been newly appointed to a position

where customer service is an especially important part of your role. If first read systematically and then used as an aid for specific problem areas, this book will provide you with the knowledge and understanding necessary to undertake your new responsibilities.

5   If you have been in your position for some time and you wish to gain further knowledge or are seeking further promotion, this book will provide you with the language and concepts necessary to develop.

6   You wish to know more about relationships with customers – after all, we are all customers in our own right. This book will provide you with an easy to follow and, in many places, humorous guide to customer service and satisfaction concepts.

7   You may be waiting for a plane, at the railway station or sitting at home – this book will provide you with insights into those organizations and people who know how to look after their customers.

Use the volume as you would a handbook: scan through first to gain the flavour of the subject and then you can home in on specifics.

GOOD AND BAD EXAMPLES

Most of the examples you will be presented with are positive. They and the individuals they represent are designed to serve as role models for good practice. We are all aware, however, from our personal experiences as customers that things are not always perfect and that sometimes situations occur where people and organizations show an apparent total disregard for the needs of the customers. Chapter 8 presents a series of case histories, with the names removed to protect the guilty, but throughout the book, the 'Howlers' sections present you with examples of poor customer service and the various 'Think Points' encourage you to think about how you would deal with similar situations to those mentioned in the text. All examples, good and bad, are based on actual events: those providing the service and their customers are real people, in real organizations, working in the real world.

Times change and we must change with them. The people we mention in this book were doing an excellent job when we spoke to them and their organizations were successful. This does not mean that it will always be so; circumstances and the business environment may become unfavourable. We are sure that, because of their positive attitude to customer service and satisfaction, the people mentioned will be able to cope with changing circumstances, but it must be borne in mind that just because you were good at one time, it doesn't follow that you always will be.

1

Knock, Knock, Who's There?

WHO IS THE CUSTOMER? THE CUSTOMER'S WANTS AND NEEDS

This book is about your relationship with your customers, so we need to begin by asking the fundamental question: 'Who is the customer?'. As this chapter also serves as an introduction to much of what follows, we shall also introduce most of the Golden Rules. You will meet them all again throughout the book.

On a simplistic level, a customer is somebody for whom you satisfy a want or need with some form of payment. The payment may be money; it may be time; it may be goodwill – but there is some form of payment. Needs are usually described as being basic, and wants refer to a concept we shall meet a number of times in this book: *added value*. A simple example will suffice to show the difference. It is early morning and you are hungry. Your need is for food. A dietician could calculate the number of calories and the balance of food that you need to function for the day, and it may be that some bread and butter with a glass of water would suffice to meet that need. However, you may desire bacon, eggs, hash browns, toast and coffee; that is your want (indeed, *desire* may be an effective synonym for *want*). A *want* is a *need* that has had value added to it. Interestingly, in the example given, the basic need may be far more healthy for you than the want. If you make breakfast for yourself, you will be your own customer, but if you visit a cafe, diner or hotel for your breakfast then another added value factor will come into play, that of *service*. Somebody else will cook and deliver your breakfast and you will be the customer. The value you place on the breakfast will then be composed of a number of items:

- the quality and quantity of the food itself
- the quality of cooking and manner of presentation
- the efficiency and friendliness of the service
- the ambience of the surroundings

Each of these will add a certain value to your breakfast, and this will probably be reflected in both the price you are asked to pay and the price you are prepared to pay.

It is quite clear that, unless you are eating in an establishment where the owner is also the cook and server, more than one person will be responsible for the provision of a successful customer interaction. You may not see the cook, you may never meet the person who orders the basic foodstuffs and ingredients – but they are just as important to the process of adding value as your server.

In order to amplify the concept of added value, let us build up a scenario. This will allow us to introduce the necessary nomenclature.

If you go to your local corner shop or delicatessen to buy a chocolate bar we have the very simple transaction shown in figure 1. This is a very simplistic view; there is no doubt that you are a customer, and if the chocolate is for you we can describe you as a special category of customer, an *end user*. Suppose, however, that you have bought the chocolate for one of your children. He or she will be the end user; you will be another category of customer, a *purchaser*.

THINK POINT

You paid for the chocolate with money. What is the nature of the transaction between yourself and your child?

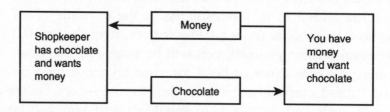

Figure 1 The nature of transactions

You may find it difficult to think of a relationship with your child using customer satisfaction language, but in providing the child with chocolate you were satisfying a need or want, and that was the basis for our definition at the start of this chapter. Suppliers also have wants and needs. In the above case a possible scenario would be:

The candy salesperson wants money.
The child wants chocolate.

Abraham Maslow, who examined motivation, talked about a hierarchy of needs, with lower level needs in the main (there are exceptions) being satisfied before those higher up. Pictorially, his hierarchy appears as in figure 2 (Maslow 1970).

In Maslow's terms, the wants we described above for the chocolate transaction are, in fact, needs as well; we need food for

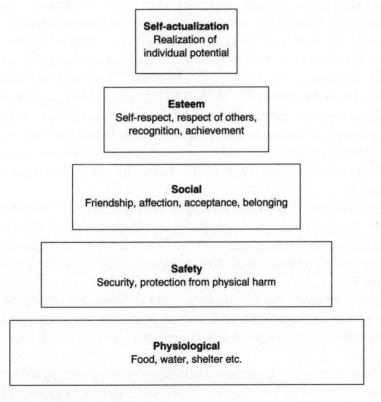

Figure 2 Maslow's hierarchy

physiological well being, money for security and affection for higher level needs.

Within the public sector it is sometimes preferable to talk about the client. This is another word for end user; we can put down our definitions as:

- SUPPLIER: somebody who 'sells' a product or service.
- PURCHASER: somebody who 'buys' a product or service and who may or may not use it directly, but becomes the next supplier in the chain.
- END USER: somebody who uses a product or service but may not necessarily have purchased it. This person could also be described as a CLIENT.

According to these definitions, the person who sells you the chocolate is also a 'purchaser' customer of somebody else, probably a wholesaler. There is a purchaser chain that ends with an end user. For convenience we can also classify customers as internal or external, a topic we will return to later in the book.

You may be having some problems with the definitions; after all, you do not 'sell' a candy bar to your child – or do you? Payment does not have to be with money; it can be with another good or service, or even with affection. Thomas Harris, in his classic book *I'm OK – You're OK* (1970), talks about psychological stroking between individuals and has introduced the world to the concept of transactional analysis. In his terms the transactions are psychological but they have many similarities with the physical transactions that occur between your customers and yourself.

Throughout this book you will be considering a number of large, medium size and small organizations. Let us look at the structure of a large organization. Traditionally, structure charts appear as a pyramid with the most senior staff at the top, as in figure 3.

However, from the customer's point of view, his or her perception of the organization will be the opposite, as in figure 4. We often talk about 'those at the sharp end' and figure 3 illustrates why this is.

While there may be many definitions of what an organization's structure exists to do, the truest is that it exists to provide those at the customer interface with the resources to satisfy the needs

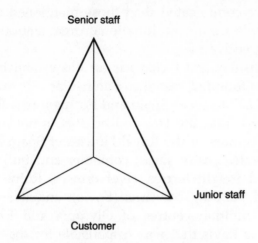

Senior staff

Junior staff

Customer

Figure 3 The organization as it sees itself

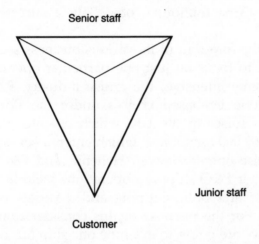

Senior staff

Junior staff

Customer

Figure 4 The organization as seen by the customer

and wants of the customer, because without customers, *any* organization is doomed to failure.

The last statement may seem too sweeping and general. You may argue that you – and indeed your organization – do not have customers in the sense of the normal usage of the word. You may call them clients, passengers, patients or even colleagues, but in the terms of the definitions at the beginning of this chapter, they are all customers and they all pay something, even if it is not money, for your service.

In our research for this book, we spoke to a large number of suppliers, purchasers and end users. The relationships are normally more complicated than those mentioned above. Let us take an example from a multinational organization operating in a highly competitive market.

P&O (Peninsular and Orient) is an old established company, having been founded as the Peninsular Steam Navigation Company in 1837 to serve Spain and Portugal (the Iberian Peninsular countries) from the UK. Indeed P&O's house flag/logo is based on the colours of the Royal Houses of Spain and Portugal. Today, it operates cruise ships, container and bulk cargo ships, passenger and freight ferries, river cruises, Rhine barges, road transport and building concerns (Bovis), and it even owns the prestigious exhibition centres of Olympia and Earls Court in London. It was Bovis that was responsible for the restoration of the Statue of Liberty in New York Harbour. P&O's turnover for 1994 was over £5989 million ($8983 million), with profits of over £238 million ($357 million) – obviously a successful group of companies.

P&O is at the forefront of its various business sectors, and it is our intention to focus on just one particular operation, one that is very customer-intensive, the cruise industry. P&O's cruising interests include US-based cruises under the Princess Cruises brand, P&O Cruises in the UK, which operates the company's flagship, the 69 000 ton *Oriana*, which entered service in 1995, the specialist cruise operator, Swan Hellenic, and P&O Holidays in Australia. Other P&O shipping operations include ferry services plus container and bulk shipping and a variety of freight and river cruises. For the purpose of this consideration of customer satisfaction, we are going to examine one ship out of the Princess fleet and some of the crew who help to add value to the product.

(All shipping information is taken from *Great Passenger Ships of the World* by Arnold Klundas, the 1994 *Berlitz Complete Guide to Cruising and Cruise Ships* by Douglas Ward, and Princess Cruises' *Information to Passengers*. This section has been adapted from work carried out for another volume in the *In Charge* series, *In Charge of Yourself*.)

Princess Cruises of Los Angeles, which was a fairly small operator, was acquired by P&O in 1974, then in 1988 P&O acquired Sitmar Cruises, which led to a large expansion of the fleet operating in the US market (we shall examine the marketing aspects of customer service later in this book, but P&O provides some useful examples of customer-focused marketing). All of the existing Sitmar vessels were renamed with the *Princess* suffix and operated under the Princess brand, while new names were allocated to those vessels then being built for Sitmar.

The Princess fleet in 1995 comprised nine vessels ranging in size from approximately 20 000 tons up to 70 000 tons. New vessels on order include one over 100 000 tons.

Major cruising areas are US West Coast–Alaska, where Princess owns hotel and railroad facilities, the Caribbean, US West Coast–Panama Canal–Caribbean, the Mediterranean and Scandinavia, with the two smallest ships, *Pacific Princess* and *Island Princess*, working their ways around the world offering a variety of cruising opportunities. As will be illustrated later, different markets and areas require different vessels.

The *Berlitz Complete Guide to Cruising and Cruise Ships* by Douglas Ward is published at regular intervals and provides a wealth of information and ratings from which a choice of cruise can be made.

Cruising is not cheap, therefore value for money is very important. Perhaps the first question to be asked is why people go on a cruise: what is it they are seeking? If the answer is connected with service, then the attitudes of the crew will be a very important factor in customer choice.

Cruising is generally very relaxing; most ships provide entertainment, but it is optional. The food is normally very good, and international rather than local in character. Once on board, you can go from place to place without having to unpack – your hotel moves with you. Most ships provide medical facilities and most cruises go to where the sunshine is. Itineraries range from the exotic – like the Amazon – the adventurous – like the Antarctic – the spectacular – Alaska and Norway – the tropical – the Caribbean and the South Seas – to the historical – much of the Mediterranean.

The disadvantages are that you are never in a place for very long, so you either have to book shore tours or not see very much, and seas can be rough at times. As mentioned previously, cruises are not cheap, and accommodation, being on a ship, may be less luxurious than in many hotels, although many staterooms/cabins at sea have private *en suite* facilities (all Princess ships are so equipped) and standards are rising.

According to the Berlitz guide, 5 410 000 people cruised in 1992, of whom 4 250 000 were from the USA, with UK citizens making up the next largest group, with 225 000. These numbers are growing and a number of new vessels are being commissioned. The growth in the market is around 10 per cent per annum.

Discussions with regular cruise passengers suggest that there are certain intangibles that make this form of holiday special, and therefore those involved in customer service on board need to understand the roots of the intangibles. As we shall see later in the book, it is often the supplementary, intangible part of a product that is of great importance to the customer. Of all intangibles and supplementaries, service is the most important.

The excellent cruise companies provide their customers with the illusion of their own personal vessel, with enough quiet places to be alone with that illusion and standards of service that are both high and personal.

Ships such as the 45 000 ton *Royal Princess*, which entered service in 1984, are just so many thousand tons of steel, so the ship cannot be the deciding factor; the organization is headquartered thousands of miles away and customers will rarely meet corporate staff, so the most important factor in achieving excellence and the personal illusion, as Tom Peters (1987) has said on many occasions, must be the people. The key to excellence must lie within the 520 or so crew members.

THINK POINT

What is it that the customer (passenger, in this case) wants?

For all passengers, the prime concern is likely to be an overall enjoyable holiday experience. This can be split down into a number of sub-areas: an interesting itinerary to meet his or her needs, high quality food, comfortable surroundings and accommodation, good entertainment, a mix of activities and convivial travelling companions.

The company will wish for supplementary income from duty free sales, bar sales, shore excursions, souvenirs and duty free items, plus – most importantly – customers who will return home and tell their relatives, friends and colleagues about their experience and thus assist in generating new business, and who will provide repeat business themselves.

Of the 1200 or so passengers on one particular voyage that we looked at, over 950 were members of 'The Captain's Circle', the Princess club for past passengers: a repeat business rate of 75 per cent. On the excellent 'Winning for Customers' course provided for all staff worldwide by British Airways, the point is made that it costs at least five times as much to gain a new customer as to keep an existing one, so high repeat business figures are a sound indication of organizational effectiveness. Indeed, one couple were spending their 1024th day on a Princess ship – three years' worth of repeat business!

GOLDEN RULE

It costs far more to gain a new customer than to retain an existing one.

In a growing market, paradoxically it is just as important to retain customer loyalty as in a shrinking market. The 10 per cent annual growth mentioned earlier will require expenditure to tap the potential new customers. A successful company will not only generate a growth in new clients but will wish to build on its existing client base; the existing customers carry far less marketing costs than new ones, and, indeed, remember another of our rules:

GOLDEN RULE

Dissatisfied customers have far more friends than satisfied ones.

Turning this on its head, your existing customers, if satisfied, will perform part of the marketing function for you by telling their friends.

THINK POINT

How important is repeat business to your organization? What percentage of your business comes from your existing customer base? Could this figure be improved, and, if so, how?

While there is a complex organization chart for a vessel such as the *Royal Princess* – indeed, the ship could be regarded as an organization in its own right – from the passenger's point of view, there are four main areas of operation, with the Captain in overall control and accountable for the first three.

Transportation/safety aspects connected with the ship

Under the direct control of the Captain, the navigation, engineering, electrical etc. staff ensure that the voyage is completed on schedule, in safety and with as little inconvenience to the passengers as possible.

Hotel aspects

Over 1200 passengers need to be accommodated and fed. One can never complain about the quantity of food offered on a cruise: eating can start at 6.00 a.m. and finish with the midnight buffet, with any number of meals and snacks in between. Laundry facilities need to be provided, staterooms kept clean and made up – indeed a whole range of housekeeping activities need to be carried out. Passengers need to acquire foreign currency, they may need medical attention, their accounts need to be kept up to date. Under the accountability of the Captain, this role falls to the purser's department, a very large department indeed.

Entertainment

Cruise ships provide a full range of entertainments and activities, ranging from quizzes and deck games to cabaret and full-scale shows. There are shore excursions to be arranged, shops to be run and photographic services to be provided. Modern cruise ships have a full entertainments team, again under the ultimate control of the Captain but organized through the Cruise Director. The Cruise Director is one member of staff whom the passengers will come to know most closely.

No fewer than 24 nationalities (12 different nationalities of passengers and 24 different nationalities of crew) were represented aboard the ship, all with their own cultural norms and needs.

Pre- and post-cruise

Passengers have to travel from home to their ship and return home again after the cruise. The vast majority of passengers will be making an air journey. So will their luggage and so, indeed, may crew who are joining or leaving the ship.

Travel to and from the ship is arranged by Princess Cruises but is not under its direct control. When a passenger who, having travelled on two different airlines, finds that his or her luggage has not arrived at the same time, goes to the purser's office, the company cannot (and, to their credit, do not) say that this is not their problem. Every effort is made to track down the luggage prior to sailing, and if it is not found immediately, toiletries and clothing vouchers are provided. There is always a problem for any organization that has to rely on third parties meetings its needs. An excellent organization will take ownership of these issues on behalf of the customer.

GOLDEN RULE

Unless you recover the situation quickly, a lost customer will be lost forever.

It may not be Princess Cruises' fault that the luggage is lost but it is its responsibility to find an acceptable solution, and if this means helping out with clothes and accessories, then so be it. The purser's staff are adept at making up wardrobes, although, as Alessandro Bologna, a purser, has pointed out, ladies' shoes are the major problem. At least the passenger has something to wear and a toiletry kit, and most luggage does turn up, although it can require considerable liaison between the ship and the airline concerned. The airlines are equally concerned, because it is their reputation that is at stake. As John McSorley, a duty manager for British Airways at London's Heathrow Airport, has remarked, 'Just because the passenger is booked on a group ticket [i.e. taking a cruise or package holiday with the ticket booked and purchased by the travel company] does not mean that they are any less your customer'. This is a good example of our purchaser/end user relationship. Indeed, the airline staff are well aware that companies like Princess Cruises are major customers themselves through the tickets that they book for their passengers, and that valuable business could be lost if the airline's service affects the quality of a holiday.

All of the organizations involved in getting the traveller to and from the ship and concerned with his or her comfort when ashore – airlines, hotels and excursion companies – need to get it right first time if the experience is to be both enjoyable and memorable, and not memorable for the wrong reason. In the case of third-party activities booked by the company, the company is likely to receive the blame if things go wrong, even if they are beyond its control.

HOWLER

On the 22nd of December (i.e. just before Christmas) a heavily delayed and diverted internal flight arrived at Bombay's domestic terminal. The flight touched down at 18.15. Three of the passengers had an onward connection to Dubai and then on to Europe. It is a 6 km taxi journey between the domestic and the international terminals. No staff from the internal airline were present to render assistance and the three missed their onward flights. This is a very busy time of the year for the airlines. Other than one hotel room between three strangers (luckily all of the same gender), no assistance was forthcoming from the duty manager of the internal airline at the international terminal. The airline had carried out its responsibilities by bringing the people to Bombay; they were on their own now. What a difference in attitude to that of the duty managers for Emirates and British Airways, who took ownership of the problem and arranged new flights for the passengers with the minimum of fuss. The delay could not be helped but the complete lack of service recovery or,

> indeed, care is likely to cost the internal carrier. It must be said that there are excellent airlines in India, offering very good customer service – JET, Damania and Modiluft spring to mind – and it is they that are prospering.

There can be tensions between the four areas. The ship may have to sail before a missing item of luggage is recovered. Indeed, passengers on shore excursions may, through their own fault, miss the ship and need to be recovered (this should not be confused with the concept of customer recovery that we shall meet in chapter 5!). Essential maintenance may require that some facilities are temporarily unavailable. Sailing times and meal times may conflict. The organization needs to function in a holistic manner. Most passengers never realize the depth and complexity of planning that occurs to ensure that the logistics work. All staff need to be *functionally competent*: the Captain needs to be an expert seaman; the chefs need to be able to cook properly; the singers need good voices; the shore excursion staff need to know about the ports of call.

The organization needs *organizational competence*: it needs to be committed to its customers; it needs systems and procedures in place to deal with foreign immigration and customs procedures, effective staff rotas and training programmes. Given the cultural mix of passengers, the entertainments and activities need to reflect this so that nobody feels left out. While functional and organizational competence should be assumed as being present, *personal competence* is a different matter. At this stage, it is necessary to give a few examples of the level of service provided by referring, with their permission, to specific individuals and their philosophies of customer service. Referring to our 'sharp end' diagram, the people we are concentrating on are not in the main the senior officers of the ship, but those with whom the customer comes into regular contact – waiters and waitresses, stewards and entertainers.

The *maître d'hôtel* on the *Royal Princess*, Renzo Rotti, who is in charge of the dining room operation, has to ensure that everybody is seated at a table that suits them. Unlike land-based hotels, dining room meal times are set, and on the *Royal Princess* they are divided into two sittings. He needs to ensure that the numbers are comparable for both sittings; this may require considerable diplomatic and negotiation skills. As Renzo says, 'a smile and a pleasant manner can cut through many potential problems'. Through his seven head waiters, he needs to ensure that the table teams, waiter and bus boy work well together. He needs to learn names, and goes around to every table every night, checking on the quality of the food and the service. He has been in the catering/service business for over 40 years, having started as a footman at Blenheim Palace. Food is one of the main attractions of a cruise, and Renzo and his team need to get it right every time if the customer is to take away pleasurable memories. Passengers cannot choose another restaurant (although the latest generation of cruise ships are installing more choices for dining).

GOLDEN RULE

The customer is not always right, but how you tell them that they're wrong can make all the difference and ultimately they do pay your wages.

Passengers have the opportunity to express a table and sitting preference at the time of booking. Sometimes they forget or they change their minds and want to sit with new friends. There is only a finite number of spare places, and Renzo's smile and accommodating manner go a long way to satisfying those passengers who require a change. Even if it is not possible, they know that everything that could be done has been done.

The bar staff and stewards have a job many of us would, at first sight, envy until we think about the long hours and, as with all the crew, the fact that you cannot avoid taking work home with you, because work *is* home. Passengers and crew, although having separate areas, are together for up to three weeks at a time; hence, the vital importance of effective customer relationships. Also, because the ship is by definition self-contained, each member of the crew is normally another member's internal customer.

We can define an *internal customer* as somebody within the organization for whom you satisfy a want or need that is required for them to satisfy their internal or external customers.

Under this definition, Renzo Rotti is an internal customer to the staff who look after the computer records showing meal preferences. When we order a drink from a steward or stewardess, we do not see the internal transactions that may occur. Samantha

Knight is a trained accountancy technician taking a two-year break and seeing the world, while her colleague, Steve Britton, spends much of his working day in the Horizon Lounge at the base of the ship's funnel. Both recognize the need to build up a relationship with the customer, and they take the informal feedback they receive very much to heart. As Samantha puts it, 'A smile may be all the encouragement you need'. They are both internal customers for the bar staff. They don't mix the drinks, but it is they who will receive the complaint if all is not to the customer's liking. Both see themselves as important sources of information. They are the people whom passengers are likely to ask, 'where are the toilets?' or 'how long is the Panama Canal?' and both stress the need for patience and a sense of humour. At times they have to go beyond their duties. Certain cruises may have a large number of senior citizens or people with disabilities. They don't just tell people where something is; if possible, they will take them. It is these little '110 per cent' actions that are remembered and that can make all the difference.

THINK POINT

Have you 'gone the extra mile' for one of your customers recently? What kind of feedback did you receive and how did you feel? What can you do to add the little extra service to your product?

Both Samantha and Steve stress a point that the Disney Corporation makes in its training programme: 'You may have been asked the same question many times today, but the person who is asking you now is asking for their first time'.

THINK POINT

Are you asked the same question again and again, or is your job such that you hear the same joke or quip many times in one day? Do you keep smiling or does your exasperation show through?

Cathy Webster, a Junior Assistant Purser, makes a very vital point – so vital that we have printed it in bold:

You have to remember that to the passenger, they are one of one, not one of 1200.

We all want to be thought of as individuals, and one of the greatest contributions you can make to your organization's customer service is to treat people as one of one, and not just as another customer. Use their names, remember their needs, smile: all of these things go a long way to providing that added extra, and it costs nothing but can gain a great deal. Look at your customer and listen; as Cathy Webster has noted, 'you can tell how somebody is feeling by the way they greet you' – be sensitive.

Given that there is now a market in the USA for 'go nowhere' cruises – seven days at sea with no ports of call – the range of entertainments offered is an important part of the customer service package.

The key staff in the entertainment product on a ship like the *Royal Princess* are the Cruise Director, the Social Hostess and the entertainers themselves.

Billy Hygate, the Cruise Director of the *Royal Princess* for part of 1995, has a background in the entertainment business: he is a very competent singer. It is his job to devise a package that will entertain a wide range of customers, in terms of both age and nationality, but still keeping within the show schedules laid down by the company. These major productions form the nucleus of the package, but the order of presentation is left to him, in consultation with the Captain. A job like Billy's is high visibility; he is seen around the ship, and passengers greet him when they see him. As an entertainer since the age of 13, he is used to being in the public eye; you might not be so used to being 'centre stage', but all those at the sharp end need to make a positive presentation of themselves. It is interesting that the Disney Corporation refers to staff as 'cast' and to their working environment as a 'stage'. You don't have to be a cruise director on a ship to be constantly seeing your customers: those working in small retailers, perhaps in a small town, and Dr Andrew Gibson, whom we shall meet later on, are all in the public eye.

THINK POINT

How do you react to being on stage? Have you ever thought of your desk or your counter etc. as being a stage?

Billy Hygate is empowered to make changes to the programme, provided it does not deviate too far from that laid down: we shall be considering empowerment and its role in solving problems for the customer later in this book. What he does before making any changes is listen to what the customers want.

GOLDEN RULE

You must listen to your customers to find out what they want.

This is a theme to which we shall return later.

Working alongside and reporting to Billy is Caroline Day, the Social Hostess. Her basic job is to carry out the Golden Rule above, while she is running quizzes, arranging parties etc. – the classic roles of a hostess. She is visible about the ship talking to the customers: as Tom Peters put it, 'Management By Wandering About' (MBWA). The role of talking to the customers must never be underestimated. It requires skill. Caroline must not be intrusive; she needs to remember a large number of names, what the last conversation with that person was about. It is a job with a great deal of autonomy and responsibility. The person who talks to a customer is the one who can solve the problem there and then without it needing to become a major issue.

THINK POINT

Are there opportunities for you to take on a 'social' role in your customer relationships? (It doesn't need to be much: a smile, a greeting and, most important, a 'listen' – most of us can give a talk if we have to, but giving a 'listen' is not so easy.) How could you improve your social and listening skills?

We all like to be entertained, and many people harbour a secret desire to be an entertainer. How do entertainers view their relationships with their customers, or audience, as common parlance would have it?

Jill Galt is a pianist/singer specializing in piano bar incidental songs and music and cabaret. In such an intimate environment, a good relationship with the customers is vital. Jill and her husband (who is also a musician) work on cruise ships on a regular basis; having the same audience night after night has advantages and disadvantages. If you don't relate to your audience, you are still stuck with having them around for quite a long time, but if all goes well, you are able to build up a good relationship. This allows Jill to greet people not only by name but with their favourite piece of music. As she points out, she makes a large number of transient relationships, but you cannot let the fact that these friendships are transient get in the way. They live on through the songs – indeed, you can buy the tape! She sees the role as being 50 per cent entertainer and 50 per cent public relations.

THINK POINT

How much of your job is task related and how much is public relations? Have you had any training or instruction in public relations?

As in all situations, there will always be the customer who doesn't like the product and insists on telling you. We shall examine this in detail later on, but for an artist like Jill, 'you just have to turn the other cheek, don't react and remember the vast majority who do like your work, but you do need to listen'. It is only by listening that you find out what people want, and criticism – if constructive – can be more useful than praise.

GOLDEN RULE

Welcome complaints; they allow for recovery.

Senior staff often grow up within the company, something that successful organizations like Emirates (Airline of the Year 1994) and British Airways encourage; they have been with the company for a long time and understand its culture and mission. Junior staff in Princess come from diverse backgrounds – a wine steward with a BA (hons) in hotel management, gaining experience for a few years; a shop assistant waiting to join the Royal Navy; a Mexican waiter sending money home. How do they achieve the necessary customer service skills?

The driving force must come from the top, from the standards set throughout the fleet by the corporate headquarters in Los Angeles, from the P&O traditions and, most importantly, when one considers that there are nine ships separated by thousands of miles, by the example set by the Captain and senior officers. Although we have concentrated on the staff at the 'sharp end', it is from their superiors that the ethos and standards of the organization come. However, it is the contribution of the junior staff that is most visible to the customer. The Captain of the *Pacific Princess* in 1994, Captain David Christie, was only too clear in conversation that it is these staff who make or break a company. They need and have adequate accommodation; they appear to be valued by the company; and they make the passenger experience not just good but excellent.

All new Princess staff follow a company induction:

1   There is a safety induction for passengers, which will assume that any crew member is fully conversant with all safety aspects, perhaps not realizing that the crew member may have just joined the ship.
2   There is a task induction, where staff are trained in what may be very new tasks.
3   There is an induction that deals with the personal competencies – what the company stands for, pride in the ship, meeting the needs of customers.

Royal Princess is just one vessel out of nine. On the Berlitz rating of 1, 1+ etc., up to 5+ stars, together with scores out of 2000, *Royal Princess* scores 5 (the lowest Princess score is 4 stars) and has a Berlitz rating of 1751 out of 2000 (the highest Berlitz rating in 1994 was 1830 for the *Royal Viking Sun*). The Princess ratings range from 1666 to 1751. These scores, given that Princess Cruises are by no means the most expensive on the market, show considerable consistency. (The source for the scores is the 1994 Berlitz *Guide to Cruising*.)

Most of us don't work on gleaming white cruise liners, but then most of us don't have to live with our customers. The understanding of who the customer is and what he or she wants and needs is common to all those who deal with either internal or external customers. Whether the organization is large or small, it will not survive without satisfied customers. In chapter 3 we will look at the issue of quality and see how large and small organizations meet their quality standards.

All of the people interviewed on the *Royal Princess* were very clear about who their customers were, both internal and external. They were also aware of the value that the supplementary products added for their external customers.

The concept of value added supplementary products is key to understanding customer satisfaction and service, as is understanding the difference between:

PRODUCT LED and CUSTOMER DRIVEN

A *product led* philosophy is one where the organization decides what it wants to make or provide and then offers it to the customer. The Ford Model T mentioned in the preface is a good example – there is very little choice. Monopoly situations often give rise to this way of thinking. We can define a monopoly as:

An organization that hasn't any competitors – yet.

This approach has advantages for the organization, because it can concentrate on what it wants to do, but the customer has very little say in meeting his or her needs.

At the opposite end of the scale is the *customer driven* approach, where the wishes of the customer determine the nature of the product or service. Not surprisingly, this philosophy is most prevalent in conditions of high competitiveness.

THINK POINT

Does your organization tend towards product led or customer driven? How much involvement does the customer have in determining the specification of what he or she is offered?

As competition grows, so organizations tend towards being more customer driven. Even the traditional bastions of the product led culture – government, health, education and social welfare – are being forced to listen to their customers and respond to their needs in an active manner as legislation and public pressure demand choice.

GOLDEN RULE

In a free market economy, never forget that the customer has a choice.

CORE AND SUPPLEMENTARY PRODUCTS

Most people can tell you what their core product is – for General Motors it is cars, for AMTRAK it is a train service, for Shell it is petroleum products – but what adds the value are the more intangible supplementary products. This is what the Chairman of JET was talking about in the preface; anybody can fly you from A to B – that is a core product – but the standards of food, in-flight entertainment and service are supplementaries. They are vitally important, because, next to price, they are the main reason why customers make the choice they do. Indeed, many products – for example, airline tickets, cars and holidays – are sold on the supplementaries; the core product is a given. If you buy a car you assume that you will be provided with a defect-free means of transportation: what the advertisers concentrate on are sunroofs, power steering, air bags etc. We illustrate this diagrammatically in figure 5.

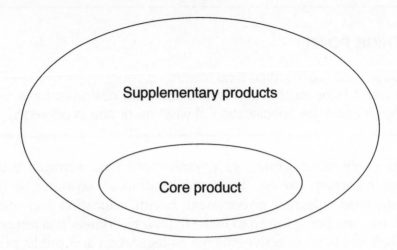

Figure 5 Core and supplementary products

CUSTOMER BEHAVIOUR

Why do your customers choose your product and service? Customer behaviour follows a pattern known as AIDA:

Attention
Interest
Desire
Action

In order to attract customers' attention, you and your products have to be known to them. This may be through advertising, but it may also be through conversation with friends and colleagues. Once attention has been gained, then – if customers feel that the product or service is right for them – their *interest* is stirred. Once people are interested, they will try to find out more about what is on offer. If they still like what they see and hear, they will begin to *desire* the product or service, and that will produce *action* to acquire it for themselves or their client.

From the customer service point of view, there are two major problems associated with AIDA.

First, stimulating demand for one product, service or even supplier tends to stimulate demand for similar offerings across the market. After the Gulf War in the early 1990s, British Airways introduced the 'World's Greatest Offer' in order to stimulate demand in a stagnant market. They stimulated demand for their own product, but at the same time they also stimulated demand for their competitors' products. The same has happened with more mundane products. An effective advertising campaign for one brand of coffee tends to produce increases in sales for all coffee manufacturers. Provided you are supplying a good level of product and customer service, this will not be too much of a problem, but you don't want to be stimulating your competitors' sales if they are likely to take trade from you. Once you have gained attention and interest, people are likely to purchase, so you must make sure that it is you that they purchase from. At the start of the home computer boom in the 1980s, Sinclair Electronics stimulated massive interest with its relatively cheap machines. Unfortunately, Sinclair could not supply enough of them and purchasers had to go elsewhere, and once there, they stayed with the competition, to the detriment and downfall of Sinclair.

Secondly, it is very easy to lose a purchase at any stage. If, having gained attention, you are unable to fulfil the customer's need for information in the 'interest' stage, you risk losing him or her altogether. Bad service at any stage after gaining attention can mean a lost customer on a permanent basis. Treat every expression of *interest* as potential *desire* and eventual *action*. The aim is to ensure that the action is with you and not with a competitor. Everybody, whether up front or behind the scenes, has a part to play. Desire without fulfilment can fade quickly. This is known as 'Buyer's Regret' in the USA. Once customers have made up their minds, the longer the wait between order and delivery, the greater the danger that they will have second thoughts. Even asking somebody to wait a few minutes while you go for further information or to get a sample can cause desire to fade, and you may find the person gone on your return. Never leave customers waiting: provide them with something to read; keep them interested.

GOLDEN RULE

If you don't look after your customers, somebody else will.

LICAL

LICAL is an acronym for the five easiest ways to lose a customer:

Lying
Ignorance
Complacency
Arrogance
Lethargy

Lying

Lying should be obvious: if you tell customers untruths about your product or service, they will not come back to you and they may well take you to court. One would believe that lying to the customer is so obviously bad practice that we are being patronizing to you by mentioning it here. However, if that were so there would be no need for the types of consumer legislation that appear to be necessary to protect the customer. Too many suppliers are prepared to risk short-term gain by making false claims about their products. It may make you one sale, but it can lose you many! Lying may not be intentional: it may come about as a person covers up for our next category, ignorance.

Ignorance

Ignorance comes in two forms: ignorance about your own product or service, and ignorance about the needs of the customer. The former might sound rather far-fetched but consider the following Howler.

HOWLER

A busy Saturday morning in a major electrical retailer. 'Excuse me, but does this video cassette recorder have a long-play function?'

'I don't know, I'll just go and look at the instruction book.'

Given what we mentioned when considering AIDA, it will be of no surprise to find out that the customer had left by the time the assistant returned.

You must know about your product or service. If you don't know, you need to make it your business to find out. New starters at Rover Cars in the UK are taken to see all of the stages of the manufacturing process, and many organizations, P&O included, now ensure that induction covers product knowledge and company culture.

You also need to have studied your current and potential customers. It is also important to look at your past customers – why aren't they customers any more? – and it is vital that you keep up to date with the latest product/service developments in your field. In high tech retail situations like the Howler above, there is always the risk that the customer might know more than you do: keep up to date.

THINK POINT

Does your organization provide regular product/service updating information and training for you? How do you ensure that you are as up to date as possible?

Complacency

Complacent organizations (or those working within them) are ones that believe they need do nothing new and that customers will keep on coming. They tend, by definition, to be product led organizations. The decline may start slowly, but as soon as competitors are seen to offer a more customer-driven approach, more and more customers desert. It is worth us adding an extra Golden Rule here: it may sound cynical, but it carries with it a great deal of truth

---

EXTRA GOLDEN RULE

Customer loyalty is only as good as the last transaction.

Put simply, the average loyal customer will forgive one mistake or one instance of bad service but not two. This concept of forgiving once before defecting to the competition has a biological analogy in genetics that you may wish to read about in Richard Dawkins' excellent book, *The Selfish Gene* (1976).

Complacency means not learning from mistakes or only learning slowly. In the highly competitive business world in which we live today, customers want fast responses, not slow or non-existent ones.

THINK POINT

How quick is your organization to respond to customer wishes? How responsive are you? Is complacency a danger in your job?

Arrogance

Workers in the field of group dynamics have discovered that one of the properties of a long-established group – and we can think of organizations as large, well-established groups – is a tendency to believe that it is rarely wrong. One of our Golden Rules is:

GOLDEN RULE

If you don't believe, how can you expect the customer to?

Yes, you must believe in your product or service, or at least convince the customer that you believe that what you offer is the best and ideally suited to his or her needs. But this needs balancing with careful objectivity.

If you begin to believe that negatives do not exist and, even worse, that you know better than the customer and let the customer see that is how you feel, then there is a danger that you will appear arrogant.

HOWLER

A medium-sized manufacturing organization had a number of clients and projects. No individual project on its own was very large, but added together they made for good business. The organization then gained a very large project. All attention was then focused on that project. After a while the other customers began to complain that they were not receiving the individual attention that had previously been a hallmark of the organization. Nobody listened; after all, they had a huge new contract that was generating good money. Soon the original customers began to go elsewhere and still nobody really bothered. However, two problems were developing:

1 The organization was becoming very dependent on the large contract, and the customer began to ask for both price reductions and extra services at reduced cost.
2 The new customer began to hear that existing customers were leaving.

Was something major wrong!

Arrogance creeps up on you. You need to make sure that you listen to your customers, big and small, constantly. If they begin to feel that you don't care any more or you are taking them for granted, you may lose them, and losing customers is like a snowball rolling down the Alps – it becomes bigger and bigger and faster and faster!

THINK POINT

Have you ever acted in an arrogant manner towards customers? Think very carefully before answering 'no'! What was their reaction?

Lethargy

HOWLER

A department store in a major US city: two sales assistants are talking behind their counter. On the other side a customer is waiting. He taps the counter top, he coughs – and he is ignored. Eventually one of the assistants deigns to serve him. No finesse, no help and – you won't be surprised – *no sale*.

Lethargy comes from demotivated staff and can stem from ignorance, complacency or arrogance: lethargy says 'we don't care about you'.

If staff understand what is happening within the organization and how their role fits in, then there is less danger of lethargy. If you know, you can care.

WHEN YOU DON'T WANT TO SEE THE CUSTOMER

Most organizations welcome customers but there are some that don't want to see them: charities, prisons, the police and even some health workers, for example. Paradoxically in these cases, repeat business may be seen by society as failure. However, if in the case of law enforcement you see society as the customer, you should ask, what does society want? Less crime. Similarly, we also want fewer ill people and more disease prevention. Therefore, if you work in a field where a lack of customers is seen as a success (there is, of course, the tension about ensuring that this success means you still have a job), then the same rules as we have considered throughout this chapter still apply; you just have to consider them in the light of your working environment.

The next chapter continues the theme of knowing your customer by looking at the 'market', and discusses why a knowledge of marketing and market forces is vital for ensuring effective customer service.

THINK POINT/ACTIVITY

The following activity is designed for you to profile your customers, both internal and external, and to think about your product in terms of core and supplementary elements. Use it to see if there are any areas for improvements.

What is your job title?

What are your key tasks?

Who are your external customers?

What do your competitors do differently?

What are your core products/services?

What are your supplementary products/services?

Talk over your ideas with your boss!

SUMMARY

This chapter has introduced most of the Golden Rules of customer service and has looked at the nature of the customer/supplier transaction, and provided definitions of *customer, supplier, client* and *end user*.

Customer behaviour has been considered using the AIDA model – *attention, interest, desire* and *action* – and the main reasons for losing customers, LICAL – *lying, ignorance, complacency, arrogance* and *lethargy* – were introduced.

2
Getting to Know You

UNDERSTANDING YOUR MARKET

A market can be described as 'the forum where customer needs and wants are satisfied'. Before the days of mass transportation and electronic communications, people had to travel to the various markets. Medieval towns and cities in Europe had markets dedicated to particular commodities – wool, grain etc. Today markets are more diverse. We have department stores that sell a large number of different products; there are factory outlet villages that sell direct to the public; there are still shops that deal in a particular product; and there are ways of purchasing products and services through mail order, the television, seat back videos on aircraft and the internet.

This chapter builds on the work of the previous one by looking at the environment within which your relationship with the customer operates. It is not designed to be a treatise on marketing or advertising, but seeks to use marketing concepts to illustrate the competitive nature of the customer–supplier relationship. Advertising is considered in so far as the advertisements for a product or service reflect the public image of that product or service. We believe that it is important for anybody involved with customer service and satisfaction to be aware of the basic marketing concepts in order to promote an understanding of the direction and workings of their organization. A number of the examples used are from the automobile and the aircraft industry, firstly because most of us have used a car or an aeroplane, and secondly because their failures and successes are well documented.

The major concepts considered within the chapter are:

* **competition**

- **the marketing mix**
- **the product/service life cycle**

Examples are taken from both the USA and UK, and from the very large to the smallest of owner-run and operated organizations.

It used to be thought that any consideration of markets only applied to the private/commercial sector. Today, all organizations need to consider their markets. Governmental organizations need to be able to promote their messages, and all across the world there has been a move away from large state-owned organizations to private ownership through the processes of liberalization and privatization. In the UK alone, since 1979, airlines, electricity, water, gas and telephone utilities, shipbuilding, steel and even banks have been returned to the private sector, and more and more competition has been introduced.

India, the former Eastern Bloc countries, and many other countries, especially in Western Europe, are looking at placing more and more commerce and industry further away from governmental control, mirroring the situation that has always been prevalent in the USA. Charities need to compete for donations, and in the UK market forces are being allowed to operate within the National Health Service.

As soon as there is competition, there is a need for knowledge of the market.

GOLDEN RULE

In a free market economy, never forget that the customer has a choice.

There are fewer and fewer monopolies in the world. In chapter 1 we defined a monopoly as:

An organization that hasn't any competitors – yet.

Other terms that you may come across are:

- DUOPOLY: **the possession of the delivery of a product or service by only two suppliers.**

- OLIGOPOLY: **the possession of the delivery of a product or service by a limited number of suppliers.**

To give practical examples, the bus service in an area may be a monopoly if there is only one operator; if there are two operators, it is a duopoly; and if there are more than two but not a large number it is an oligopoly. Monopolies thrive in *command* economies, where the decisions about who can supply what are decided centrally. This is not always a bad thing; too much competition can be unhealthy, as we shall see later. AMTRAK in the USA, which will be considered in the next chapter, is the example of a monopoly; it provides all of the long-distance passenger rail transport in the USA. AMTRAK is an interesting (and, for the USA, unusual) example of a monopoly, because the organization was formed to prevent the total collapse of a service that had a large number of suppliers, most of whom were in dire financial circumstances. *Demand* economies, where the market, through customers, decides on the number of suppliers, are more likely to produce non-monopoly situations.

The car ferry market between Dover and Calais is primarily a duopoly, with two big operators, Stena Sealink and P&O European Ferries; the introduction of Le Shuttle and Eurostar trains through the Channel Tunnel is adding substantial extra competition.

Most of us will probably recognize the oligopoly situation where there are a few fairly large players in the market; for example, London to New York air flights, major supermarket chains in the UK. The oil industry is an often quoted example with a few very well-known names, including Shell, Exxon and Mobil, supplying gasoline products to large areas of the world.

We would like to introduce a new word:

- FREEOPOLY: **where there are no restrictions, save those imposed by the potential demand, on the number of possible suppliers.**

In other words, in a freeopoly there is no restriction on the number of potential suppliers of a good or service; the actual number of organizations involved is determined by the number of potential customers. Monopolies, duopolies and oligopolies are constrained by the laws of most countries (anti-trust legislation in the USA;

the Monopolies and Mergers Commission plus European Union rules in the UK) from fixing prices. However, common sense tells us that if the public will pay x for the product or service from one supplier, they will not pay much more than x for it from another supplier unless there is considerable added value, as introduced in chapter 1. Thus, within any given area, the price for similar products and services will be roughly the same.

To take an example, a small town can only support a limited number of pharmacies; the only restriction on that number is the market. Too few and the demand will not be supplied; too many and there will not be enough business to support all of the suppliers. Sooner or later the weakest will either close or merge with one of the stronger suppliers. The optimum number is determined by the market. There is as near to true competition as possible. The danger of a monopoly, duopoly or even an oligopoly is that the participants can fix the prices at an artificially high level. In a freeopoly, prices are determined by the market. Most situations tend to evolve away from a freeopoly because of the natural inclination of organizations to grow and merge with or take over previous rivals.

THINK POINT

Consider the organization you work for. How many other suppliers of the same product or service are there in competition with you? Does the geographic spread of the competitors affect you?

Geographic spread becomes more and more important as your customers become more and more mobile. Shops that used to be in the centre of towns are able to move to cheaper land on the outskirts because more and more of the customers have their own transportation, and where they don't the supplier may well provide a free bus service.

New technologies, e.g. television shopping and the use of the internet, may also be considered under a geographic heading. After the opening of the Liverpool and Manchester Railway in 1830, the world's first commercial passenger carrying railway, rapidly followed by the first 13 miles of the Baltimore and Ohio in the same year, people were no longer restricted to the immediate area of their homes. This had dramatic implications for patterns of employment and purchasing. The need to attend an annual or biannual market disappeared, and with mobility came the ability to 'shop around'; with that came increased competition.

In the main, competition increases with the number of suppliers, and as there are fixed limits to what we will pay for a product or service, then the degree of customer satisfaction becomes an important part of gaining market share.

WHAT KIND OF BUSINESS ARE YOU IN?

This may sound like a very simplistic question but many organizations have run into problems because they have not asked it. Billy Hygate and Alessando Bologna from P&O (Princess), whom we met in the previous chapter, were very clear: they were not in the shipping business, they were in the vacation business. In the 1950s and 1960s US Railroads believed that they were in the railroad business. They were not: they were in the 'moving people across a continent' business. As we shall see in the next section, you must keep an eye not only on the competitors within your perceived business area but also on those who may become entrants, either directly or by providing a substitute product or service that meets your customer needs.

GOLDEN RULE

You must listen to your customers to find out what they want.

Princess customers do not necessarily want a cruise; they may want a vacation, with all the supplementary products that that entails. There are plenty of other suppliers of vacations, which may or may not include a cruise element.

> **GOLDEN RULE**
>
> If you don't look after your customers, somebody else will.

Across the English Channel, P&O European Ferries and Stena Sealink are no longer in the business of shipping; they are in the business of moving cars, lorries, coaches and people from the UK to France and vice versa. If we look at how you can travel from London to Paris, there are an increasing number of possibilities, involving air travel, rail, coaches, ships, hovercraft, SEACAT and the Channel Tunnel. The airlines do not provide competition to the vehicle customers (although they did try in the 1950s with Silver City and the Channel Airlink) but the ferry operators can no longer be concerned only with ferry operations; there is a new competitor that does not use ferries. Hence, they need to spell out the attractions of their product: duty free sales, eating facilities and the opportunity to rest.

> **THINK POINT**
>
> What do your customers actually want when they come to you?

COMPETITION

Michael Porter provided an interesting model to help to explain the nature of business competition (figure 6).

Competition between existing suppliers

As would be expected, the greatest competition comes between the current players in a particular market. Even where prices are very much the same, there is competition on levels of service, supplementary products and geographic provision. It is important, however, that even well-established organizations keep a careful eye on the various other options/threats that may

Figure 6 Competitive forces

occur, as well as considering what the established competition may do to enhance their market share.

New entrants

The provision of some products and services has very high barriers to entry indeed, and this may make new entrants very few and far between. You need considerable cash resources to set up a transatlantic airline, as Richard Branson (whom you will read about later in this book) has done with Virgin, and even if such barriers can be overcome, you still have to establish your credibility in the workplace and may face intense pressure from existing suppliers. The problems Virgin believed that it faced have been analysed by Martyn Gregory in his book *Dirty Tricks – British Airways' Secret War against Virgin Atlantic* (1994). Whether you conclude that Virgin was a recipient of dirty tricks or whether BA was legitimately defending its markets is irrelevant in the context of this book; what is important is the fact that new entrants have considerable hurdles to overcome, especially if they present an out and out challenge to established providers. A new shop opening in competition may produce a price cutting bonanza for the customer and behind the scenes activity that can border on the illegal; it's a hard world out there!

If the organization is big enough and rich enough, it can enter a new market by buying an existing player. Although this strategy may seem attractive, the buying organization may not have the expertise, culture and knowledge to operate successfully in that particular market environment. Peters and Waterman, in their book *In Search of Excellence* (1982), talk about successful companies 'sticking to the knitting', i.e. staying close to what they do well. In the 1920s, automobile makers like Ford believed that it would be relatively easy for them to enter the aircraft making business: it wasn't – Ford only made one product, the Ford Trimotor, and then left the market to those who understood it. The skills required for plane making were in fact very different to those needed for the automobile industry. On the other hand, Disney has proved quite adept at moving into new markets where these are complementary to its main market. In addition to the theme parks, Disney operates hotels, retail outlets both within and outside the USA, and even a cruise line.

THINK POINT

How easy would it be for a new organization to enter your field of operations? What equipment, expertise etc. would it need to acquire?

It used to be thought that some areas of business/service were immune to new entrants, e.g. government provision and services, but experience with privatization and market testing in the UK has shown that even those services previously supplied by national and local government can be entered by the private sector, e.g. refuse/garbage collection, school meals and social service provision.

Re-entry

Organizations that were in the market and have left it but still possess expertise and a 'memory' by customers may pose a threat of re-entry. As demand ebbs and flows, British Airways re-enters markets; Virgin, having sold its original business, a record label, was talking in 1995 about a possible re-entry.

Re-entry is more likely to occur where there are fewer problems about buying expensive plant or where the organization can use its cash resources to buy out one of the remaining suppliers or, as in the case of an airline, where it already possesses all of the necessary hardware.

Re-forming

Re-forming occurs when a competitor moves out of the market but sells on its expertise and plant to another company, which can then take its place in the competitive situation without the major barriers to entry that would normally occur. In the early 1990s, DAF, the Dutch truck maker that in 1987 had taken over the truck-making section of the recently privatized British Leyland, sold the UK operation via a management buyout. The UK company was thus able to become a player in its own right very quickly, because the plant was already in operation.

Substitutes

After the Second World War, there was intense competition between the various US railroads operating transcontinental services, just as the shipping companies introduced new and more luxurious tonnage on the lucrative North Atlantic routes between Northern Europe and the Mediterranean and the eastern seaboard of the USA. The UK, the USA, the Netherlands, France, the Scandinavian countries and Italy introduced considerable new tonnage, and competition between Cunard, United States Lines, French Line, Holland America, Norwegian America and the Italian Line was intense. Yet when Boeing introduced the 707 jet airliner into commercial service with Pan Am on 26 October 1958, the writing was on the wall for the shipping companies. Although the British-built Comet, introduced in 1952, was the world's first commercial jet aircraft, the 707 was the first successful model, carrying over 150 passengers compared with the Comet's initial 44 (later stretched to 94) in the Comet 4B. Cunard and the other shipping companies were no longer in the shipping business and the US railroads were no longer in the railroad business; they were in the 'mass transportation over a long distance' business, and the new jet airliners could do the job much faster: a classic example of substitution. The shipping companies looked for new markets within the cruising market, but ships designed for the 'liner' trade were not really suitable for the vacation market, and many of the companies collapsed and their vessels were laid up. The railroads could not compete at all and eventually, in 1971, all long-distance passenger trains in the USA came under the AMTRAK banner (see chapter 3) and the route network was severely cut.

However, life appears to go around in circles, and the railways in both Europe and the USA are now challenging the airlines. The flight from London (Heathrow) to Paris (Charles de Gaulle) takes a mere 35 minutes but the airports are a long way from the city centres, and there is the time taken to check in. Eurostar trains using the Channel Tunnel complete the journey in three hours, city centre to city centre. In a similar vein, by using newer equipment AMTRAK has gained 33 per cent of the market share between Washington, DC and New York by offering a city centre to city centre service in just over three hours.

Bargaining power

Depending on the monopoly–freeopoly situation, suppliers and customers have varying degrees of bargaining power.

In general, a supplier wants to supply the minimum acceptable quality at the highest possible price, while the customer wants the highest possible quality at the lowest possible price.

If the supplier has a monopoly, it can demand a higher price. If you have a monopoly, you can normally demand a higher price from your customer. In a free market economy, there is a point of quality below which a customer will not drop, regardless of the price. Indeed, because customers often (wrongly, in many instances) equate price with quality, too low a price may send the wrong messages.

The more suppliers of goods and services to your organization there are for a given product or service, the more you can force the price down and the quality up. The more competitors you have, the more likely it is that your prices will need to come down while your quality needs to be as high as possible.

In recent years, companies have sought closer relationships with their suppliers, offering them training and making them a full part of the manufacturing/service process. This has advantages for both sides in that the supplier has a greater degree of guarantee of work, but, on the other hand, the supplier then becomes tied to the fortune of the contracting organization. Chapter 6 will consider the concept of 'value chains' between suppliers and customers.

THE MARKETING MIX

In its original form, the marketing mix looks at four factors:

- Product
- Price
- Promotion
- Place

These have been refined by Kotler to comprise:

- Customer value
- Cost
- Communication
- Convenience

We will use both these ideas side by side.

Product/customer value

Both in this chapter and in chapter 1, we have considered some of the factors relating to the product. In sophisticated society, you are not just buying a car, a television set or an ocean voyage but the supplementary products that surround it, e.g. ambience, service and, of increasing importance, after sales service. As the goods and services supplied by differing organizations become more and more alike, then it is the supplementaries that affect the final buying decision.

Products and services go through a life cycle from birth to decline, and it is important for you to be aware of this life cycle in order to understand the behaviour of your customers.

Life cycles can be short, as in the fashion industry or some of the more esoteric products that appear – for example, hula hoops – or those linked to other products – Batman accessories, Power Rangers and the vast range of spin-offs from other films and TV series – or they may be very long, the Boeing 747 and KitKat chocolate bars being good examples.

The classic (and, we believe, too simplistic) view of the product life cycle is shown in figure 7. As we intend to build on this model, we will only give a brief description of each stage.

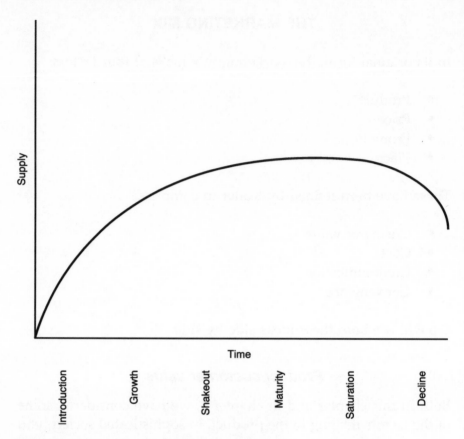

Figure 7 Product life cycle (simplified)

Introduction

In order to simplify this study, let us assume that there is a new invention. At the moment it is not available, but the inventing organization believes that it will be successful.

At the point of introduction, this organization is the only player in the market, although others may be working on a similar product. There are considerable advantages in being the first into the market, but there are also some disadvantages.

Earlier in this chapter we looked at the Comet airliner. This was the first commercial jet airliner in service and in theory should have given its makers, De Haviland, a considerable advantage. As it was, it was too small for viable service and suffered from a hitherto unknown form of metal fatigue, which caused a series of accidents, thus denting airline and public confidence. Boeing, which came into the market with the 707 at a later date, was able to learn from the teething problems of the Comet, and delivered a product that, in the words of Eddy, Potter and Page (1976), 'could support itself both financially and aerodynamically'. In Boeing's case, being second proved to be an advantage, not a disadvantage. Boeing's great rival, the Douglas Aircraft Corporation (now McDonnell Douglas), had as part of its philosophy:

'Never be the first by whom the new is tried, nor the last to cast the old aside.' (Quoted in Eddy, Potter and Page, 1976)

In the Western world, Douglas was third into the market with the DC8 and never caught up with Boeing. Boeing built 917 civil 707s; Douglas only built 556 DC8s. Of the smaller jetliners that followed, the UK built 117 Tridents (introduced in 1962), Boeing a massive 1832 versions of the similar Boeing 727, introduced in 1963, and Douglas 976 DC9s, introduced in 1965. Boeing seems to have done very well out of being second into the market. Its biggest gamble came with the introduction of the 'jumbo', the Boeing 747, in 1969, where it was the first into the market. Nobody has risked the capital required to follow Boeing into the very large commercial airliner market, and its major rival in the mid-1990s, Airbus Industrie, is a consortium formed from companies in several European countries. Boeing claims that Airbus is subsidized and does not therefore act as a true competitor in the free market sense of the word.

If at introduction our inventor can make sufficient impact, a long-lasting set of advantages can occur. If the product is of high quality, then customer loyalty can be enhanced and subsequent purchases will be of the inventor's product. Repeat business is a very important market indicator, and organizations need a range of products to offer both existing and new customers. Existing customers can be encouraged to trade up to new replacements. Of equal importance is making the product synonymous with your name. Many Britons 'Hoover' the floor, but the vacuum cleaner they use may have been made by any one of a number of manufacturers; the verb 'to Hoover' has entered the language and provides free advertising and reinforcement for the Hoover company each time it is used.

Growth
Our inventor has been successful and the product is in the marketplace and selling well. If you are involved in a service environ-

ment, then change 'product' to 'service', and 'selling well' to 'in demand'.

As the success is seen, others will enter the market. If a product or service is very successful, it is often the case that demand will be greater than supply, and this will allow others to enter the market with similar products, having taken due note of patents. Thus, as the market grows, the number of supplying organizations increases. Growth markets are often characterized by a large number of small organizations.

Shakeout

As growth begins to peak, the weaker organizations leave the market. Demand is reaching a plateau and the tendency is for the smaller organizations to merge or be taken over by one of the bigger existing players, or for a large organization to use the shakeout to acquire an entry into a new market. P&O acquired Princess Cruises at this point in the Princess product life cycle, when it was having difficulty establishing its own identity in the USA west coast cruise market. Smaller organizations are vulnerable at this time to raids by cash rich predators.

In the late 1980s, Kent County Council in the UK put its school cleaning to outside contract. Initially there was a large number of small firms cleaning a few schools each, but within a few years there was a smaller number of larger firms, which had acquired the smaller ones.

Larger organizations, it is claimed, can produce at lower cost and can benefit from economies of scale; what they have to be careful of is that they do not reduce quality and service along with costs. Service is a very important part of the product, and there is evidence that customers will pay that little bit more for good service and higher quality.

Maturity

As growth slows, the market becomes more mature, possibly dominated by fewer but larger suppliers. Entry is difficult, because the existing suppliers will know the market well and will have developed customer loyalty. It requires true entrepreneurship and considerable resources to break into a mature market, Richard Branson's Virgin Atlantic is one of the rare examples.

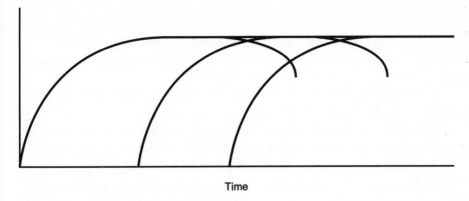

Time

Figure 8 Product succession

THINK POINT

Consider your major products and services. Are you in a growth or a maturity situation? How has this affected the number and size of your competitors?

Our inventor now has a number of competitors and demand has begun to reach saturation.

At this stage, organizations need to be in a position to bring new products, or adaptations of existing products, to the marketplace.

In the automobile market, a number of versions of each vehicle are normally introduced over time, with a completely new model being introduced every so often.

The product life cycle for the Ford medium-sized automobile market in the UK over the past few years is shown in figure 8.

It can be seen that each model has been timed to come out at the end-of-maturity point for the previous one, with the Cortina giving way to the Sierra, which in turn gave way to the Mondeo. Without a succession of new products, customer loyalty can disappear very quickly.

GOLDEN RULE

If you don't look after your customers, somebody else will.

Looking after customers means looking after their future needs as well as their current ones.

All of these concepts apply as much to internal customers as to external ones. Your internal customers will want new products and services from you. There may not be internal competition as such but some organizations, especially within the public sector in the UK, have been empowered to look outside of the organization for the provision of certain services, thus creating a more dynamic market within the organization. Whereas, perhaps, personnel services, finance and purchasing were always supplied by the organization through a central function, in future departments may be free to shop around.

Saturation and decline
When the market is saturated, supply exceeds demand, possibly because of changing tastes. As demand drops, so profits shrink and competition becomes even fiercer. As decline sets in, players leave the market or are forced out, or old products are removed from the product portfolio. If you are buying an automobile and you don't want the latest model, this can be a good time to buy because the manufacturers will cut prices to clear stocks and free up production facilities.

For an airliner the product life cycle is measured in years or even decades; for the latest fashion it may be measured in weeks, but you need to know that it exists and that just because a product or service is in demand today does not mean that it will be required next year or even next week.

One of the most dramatic illustrations of the product life cycle is the facsimile machine, the fax. Virtually unknown at the beginning of the 1980s, there was hardly an office in the world that did not have fax facilities by the 1990s. Indeed, the market for straightforward commercial fax machines was probably saturated by 1995 but, as we shall see in the next section, clever marketing has produced a rejuvenation.

THINK POINT

How easy is it for you to relate your products or services to positions on the product life cycle? How might the organization rejuvenate a product or service?

Most models of the product life cycle lead from saturation into decline, but in the following pages we want to present you with an alternative and, we believe, more realistic model, which we have called 'The Dynamic Product Life Progression', *dynamic* because it provides for a series of alternatives, and *progression* because there is life after apparent decline for many products.

Dynamic product life progression
This concept is slightly more complex than the simple product life cycle model, and we can use a slightly different graph with two decision points (figure 9).

When a product or service first enters the market, there always seem to be some people who must have the latest. Thus, while initial take-up figures may be very encouraging, they may not

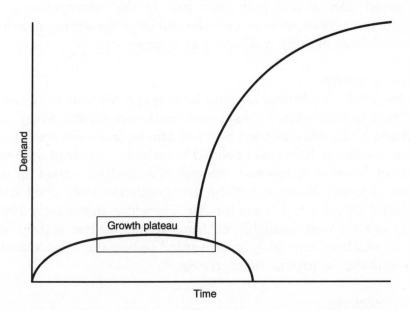

Figure 9 Dynamic product life progression – growth phase

point to a continuation of success. Demand may plateau while the bulk of the potential customer population makes up its mind. Some of the more esoteric products of the technological age (electric bicycles, the electric mini-mini car etc.) seem never to pass this point. If the product is acceptable to the mass of potential buyers, the growth phase is resumed; if not, then the product will go into decline. The critical success factor for any new product or service is whether demand picks up after a short time at the growth plateau.

The next adaptation to the simple product life cycle model can occur at the shakeout phase. It is possible that one supplier or product gains such an ascendancy as to *blastout* its competitors. Examples of this have happened in the video cassette market, with VHS blasting out Betamax, in the computer market, with the Windows operating system gaining the major market share, and in the UK satellite television market, with the major dominance of BSkyB.

The final adaptation to the classic model occurs towards the end of saturation and the beginning of decline. As we shall see from the examples, not all products have to enter a decline phase: there are alternatives (figure 10).

There are six possibilities, and it is feasible that by listening to your customers and passing their thoughts on, you can help to avoid decline and play your part in the rejuvenation of a product or service, or even help the launch of something new but derived from existing products and services.

Residual markets
In the 1960s, the British Leyland Mini was a revolutionary small car that carried with it considerable customer loyalty. Many UK citizens had a Mini as their first car. The replacement, the Metro (now the Rover 100), was intended to serve the whole of the Mini market. There was, however, enough of a residual market for the Mini to justify Rover restarting the production line, albeit with reduced capacity and fewer models. Therefore, in the early 1990s both models were available, catering for similar but slightly differing markets. Enough people wanted to buy the Mini to make it profitable for production to continue.

Niche markets
Niche markets are small and specialized. They develop either by

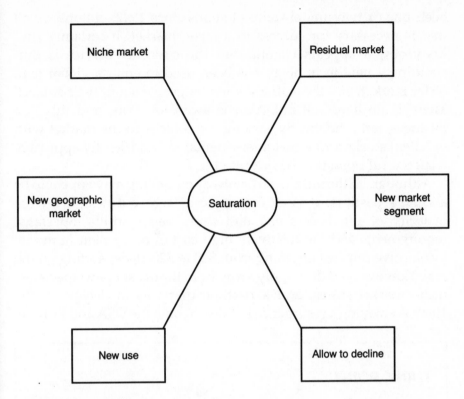

Figure 10 Dynamic product life progression – decline and alternatives

being set up especially to cater for that market or by a larger company selling off part of its product/service portfolio. Because niche markets are small, they often don't have the economies of scale that larger organizations require and may not fit in to corporate plans. Selling an apparently loss-making product to somebody who is prepared to put in the hard work that a niche market requires can be a better alternative than the product leaving the market altogether.

The Red Caboose on East 45th St in New York is a good example of a niche market. Under the ownership and management of Alan Spitz, this basement cornucopia caters for the model railroad enthusiast. Large toy shops will sell you a train set, but only a shop like the Red Caboose can offer you that elusive part needed to complete your collection. There are a large number of stores selling toys in New York, but even a borough the size of Manhattan can support only three specialist niche market model railroad shops. The Red Caboose, on a street where there have been one or two model railroad shops since 1942, epitomizes all that is necessary for success in a niche market. It certainly isn't luxurious; it appears chaotic; but the customer service is outstanding – new technology has been used to enter a global mail order market, and the staff are knowledgeable about their subject. There is no hard sell but Alan is aware of costs, and this is a business, not a hobby. By carving out a niche in the market with excellent stocks and a customer-orientated and friendly approach, a successful operation has resulted.

Although, to the uninitiated, railway modelling may appear to be a child's pastime, it is in fact quite a large business, with the majority of purchasers *and* end users being adults. Specialist requirements and the relatively high cost of equipment (a model locomotive can cost anything from $20 to $2000, depending on the scale) have moved the supply away from the toy shops to specialist, niche market stores, and a pastime that was in decline in the 1960s is enjoying a resurgence in sales, in both the USA and Europe.

THINK POINT

Look around your neighbourhood. Can you find examples of suppliers catering to a niche market? How far away is the next supplier?

There are niche market stores catering for everything from fishing tackle to second-hand books to clothes for large people. The search for niche market stores formed part of the *Yellow Pages* advertising in the UK in the 1990s: if you need a copy of an out-of-print book, look up second-hand booksellers. Niche market suppliers fulfil an important need, not just for products but also for services, and they also enliven our lives by catering for the more esoteric.

New geographic markets
A product that is in decline in one area could have a future in another. One of the classic examples of this is a British-built automobile of the early 1960s, the Morris Oxford. Obsolete in the UK market, this vehicle is now manufactured in India as the Hindustan Ambassador. The Proton vehicles built in Malaysia

are an older Mitsubishi product. A new geographic market can revitalize a product and allow the original organization to set up profitable joint ventures and partnerships at low costs, because all of the problems with the product and service will have been identified and dealt with a long time ago.

New market segments
Earlier in this chapter we considered the facsimile machine and the fact that the commercial market was becoming saturated. The manufacturers and the telephone companies started marketing the fax machine as a domestic product in the middle of the 1990s. Thus, demand has been re-stimulated. The television market was originally a 'one per household' but now smaller models are available for the bedroom, the kitchen and even for boats! Homes used to have one telephone; now many have two or three, all stimulating demand and widening the market into a new segment. Different markets have different needs, but whatever the market, *you* have a role to play.

THINK POINT

How many televisions and telephones do you have at home? Has the number increased over the years? If 'yes', why did you decide to buy extra products?

GOLDEN RULE

You must listen to your customers to find out what they want.

If you don't listen to the customer, you are in danger of creating products and services that nobody actually wants:

HOWLERS

After the Second World War, the designers at the Ford Motor Company in the USA designed and brought to market what they believed was the perfect automobile, with all the latest technology: the Ford Edsell. The trouble was the customers didn't like it.

To compete with the Boeing 707 (see earlier), the Vickers Company in the UK, backed by the government, spent a great deal of money developing the VC10 airliner, which entered service in 1964. Again, the trouble was, nobody really asked the customers what they wanted – only the then state-owned British Overseas Airways Corporation (BOAC) and the Royal Air Force could be persuaded to buy them.

A British local authority intended to open a city centre farm (a laudable idea for urban children). The only problem was that the city had two of the largest livestock markets in the country and the city centre was only four miles from the countryside.

Comments from customers can be instrumental in discovering new segments and, as we shall see in the next section, new uses.

New use
Products that used to be used for baking are now used for cleaning refrigerators! One way of stimulating demand for a declining product is to find a new use for it. Redundant British buses, no longer suitable for the rigours of the rush hour, appear as sight-seeing vehicles on the streets of New York. Horse brasses are used for decoration; the blacksmith may have fewer horses to shoe, but can make profits producing ornamental gates. The list is endless.

Decline
Some products and services have, of course, outlived their useful-ness. New developments and customer expectations have changed the market. In these cases, a swift end is better than a long drawn out one; you don't want a declining product affecting your image.

Customer value
This is the term that Kotler (1980) uses instead of 'product'. It reflects the fact that it is not the product *per se* that customers buy or use, but what they perceive that product to be and how they

value it. The Ford Edsell was a good product, technically: it just lacked customer value.

Price/cost

A five-dollar bill, a twenty-pound note or a hundred-rupee note has no intrinsic value; the value is that which the person who uses it ascribes to it.

THINK POINT

You see a great work of art and are told that it is worth millions but you think that it is awful. Who is right and who is wrong?

The answer is that if you don't like it, it is worth nothing to you unless you can barter it for something else or keep it until its value increases, so that you can sell it to somebody who does value it.

THINK POINT

How much is your home worth?

Assuming that you own your home (if you don't then the answers relate to your landlord), there are a number of possible answers:

- how much you paid for it
- how much it would cost to rebuild it
- how much you could sell it for

The last amount is the nearest to the truth: the value of any product or service is only that which a customer is prepared to pay. You may have the best product or service in the world, but if the price is deemed too high, then you will have few customers who are prepared to pay. Conversely, if the price is too low, questions may be asked about quality.

Price is what you charge for your product or service, and all products and services have a price attached to them. In government it may be the taxpayer who provides the resources indirectly, but nothing comes for free.

The price is built up by looking at all the costs that go into the provision of the product or service: those that are fixed (you would have to pay them whether you made one or one hundred items, or serviced one or one hundred people); those that are variable (these include materials that you need more of as you make more product); overhead costs (heat, light, marketing and distribution); the profit you wish to make; and what the market will bear. If you wish to read more about costs, we recommend that you read another volume in the *In Charge* series, *Managing Finance and Information* by Cartwright et al. The difference between your costs and the price the customer is prepared to pay represents your margin or profit.

If you work in the public sector, the word 'profit' may not apply, but profit is the added value that you receive over and above your costs. In situations where money does not change hands, profit could be considered in more subjective terms. For example, schools do not make a profit but they should add value; charities may see profit in terms of alleviating distress or saving lives; hospitals may be able to generate extra income to allow improved health care facilities to be installed. In balance sheet terms, a company has made a profit when it has more assets at the end of an accounting period than at the beginning. In educational terms, a school or college could have made a 'profit' if the pupils were more capable at the end of a term or a semester than they were at the beginning. Equating such ideas from the private sector into the public and voluntary sectors has proved difficult, but it is not impossible, given some lateral thinking.

THINK POINT

Whatever sector you work in, how can you measure your profits? In other words, how can you tell if your assets have increased? (Remember you do not have to use financial measures.)

Branding
Customers relate as much to brand names as to products. Brands make for customer loyalty, and there is a perception that certain brands are of better quality and value than others. But all is not always as it seems. Many electrical items, including TVs, radios and CD players, are made generically, i.e. by one manufacturer, often in the Far East, and then branded by the suppliers with their own labels.

HOWLER

A lady changed her radio cassette player, bought from one large chain of suppliers, to another. She believed that the new purchase was much better than the original. However, the changes were purely cosmetic: it was the same model under a different brand and with coloured instead of plain black buttons. She went to a different shop, but that too was part of the same chain, only operating under a different brand. Nobody had the heart to tell her!

Brands can be so powerful that they will be kept even after a takeover. When Carnival Cruises took over Holland America Line in 1989, it not only kept the names of the ships, but that of the company as well. Holland America had an excellent reputation and appealed to a different set of customers than the normal Carnival product. By keeping the brand, Carnival was able to tap into Holland America's brand loyalty.

Wherever you work within your organization, you need to ensure that you know what your products and services are and how they are branded; as we shall see in the next section, you can be one of the best advertisements.

Promotion/communication

Organizations spend large sums on advertising. If you have the right product at the right price, it is pointless if nobody knows about it. Promotion, including advertising, lets people know and – often just as important – keeps the product and service in their minds. You have two roles to play:

1 You need to know the promotions that your organization has under way so that you anticipate customers' requests and queries.
2 The way you deal with customers can be an advertisement itself.

Remember:

GOLDEN RULE

Dissatisfied customers have far more friends than satisfied ones.

But all customers talk to their friends and colleagues and tell them about good and bad products and services. Personal recommendations are very important in purchase decisions.

Kotler prefers the term 'communication' to 'promotion' because communication is a two-way process that allows customers to give you feedback. All of your interactions with customers, whether face to face, on the telephone or by letter, are communications; the way they are handled can promote your product or service and give signals about the type of organization you work for. Communications with the customer are covered in more detail in chapter 5.

Place/convenience

Does your customer come to you, or do you go to your customer?

Not all transactions take place on the supplier's premises, and recent years have seen a move towards making the provision of products and services convenient to the customer. The Red Caboose operates a worldwide mail order system – it would be very inconvenient if you had to visit the centre of New York every time you needed a small part for your model railroad. Mark Bryant, an assistant librarian for Buckinghamshire County Council in the UK, has worked hard at making library services convenient, not just through travelling libraries but also by making the in-library facilities more easily accessed, with user friendly computer search facilities, and through listening to the customer. The library now competes with high street video hire stores and has recently moved into the lending of CD-ROM software: all by listening to customers and attending to their convenience. It may be more difficult for you, but it is customers who matter.

New technologies offer exciting prospects, especially for the delivery of services. With domestic video conferencing through Windows on a PC, a whole range of consultancy opportunities in the health, financial advice and educational markets are being opened up.

THINK POINT

What can you or your organization do to make things more convenient for the customer? How much extra effort and resources would it really take?

Making the effort to aid convenience to the customer sends a very strong message about how you view your customers.

SUMMARY

This chapter has looked at the way in which a knowledge of marketing concepts can aid your knowledge of customer behaviour.

The product life cycle and the dynamic product life progression models allow you to understand the way in which products are introduced, and the marketing mix has presented you with the main factors affecting choice.

This chapter has concentrated on the product or service as that is what the customer acquires, however, a product without service or a service without customer service is unlikely to succeed.

3
Great
Expectations

GETTING IT RIGHT THE FIRST TIME

This chapter is about excellence and quality. These are the factors that can set your product or service apart from your competitors. In the 1980s, the role of quality assurance increased and many companies set up quality assurance departments. This can be a danger because quality is the business of everybody in the organization and cannot be vested in a particular department.

The chapter considers what is meant by quality and excellence, how it manifests itself at the customer interface and what it is that you can do to maintain and increase the quality and excellence of your product and service.

GOLDEN RULE

In a free market economy, never forget that the customer has a choice.

As disposable incomes increase, so does the wish for a higher quality of service or product without a major increase in cost. Successful organizations are ones that can deliver the highest standards within the limits of what the customer can afford. Quality does not have to be expensive but it does have to reflect high value for money.

Raffles Hotel in Singapore is renowned throughout the world, both for its reputation for quality and for its historical associations since its establishment over a century ago. It was designated a national monument in 1987.

Indeed, Raffles was recently refurbished and the senior management spent a considerable time in brainstorming a new mission statement, which now reads:

> Raffles is Singapore's Great Historic Hotel, delighting patrons with many memorable experiences.

Each of the words in the statement is carefully chosen and is filled with significance. Indeed, Mr Tommy Ng, the Director of Personnel at Raffles, is understandably proud of the fact that every employee knows and understands what the mission statement is and what it stands for.

Training programmes are linked to the mission in that there are two very clear strands:

- 'Great Historic Hotel', in which staff are given a thorough understanding of the historical background of the hotel.
- 'Delighting patrons with many memorable experiences', in which the importance of excellence and of getting it right first time is ingrained into the entire workforce.

THINK POINT

Do you know your organization's Mission Statement? What does it mean to you?

The Mission is usually a broad statement of intent about what the organization wants to do, and it generally gives some indication of the values that an organization has. So here, the Raffles mission statement quite clearly shows the value that the organization attaches to the hotel's history, while at the same time it states quite unequivocally its commitment to giving the customer satisfaction.

It is often extremely difficult for staff who work in an organization to understand where they are going if there is no mission statement.

In fact, it could be argued that there are only two types of organization:

Those going somewhere . . .
and those going nowhere!

THINK POINT

Which type is your organization?

GOLDEN RULE

If you don't believe, how can you expect the customer to?

At Raffles, so perfect is the attention to detail in each respect that nearly all of the front-line staff are male. This is not because of anything to do with equality or inequality of opportunity, but because this is how Raffles has always been and people come here to experience it as it always was.

Similarly, the whole atmosphere of Raffles is timeless. Once within the inner courts, you could indeed feel that you were in any era throughout its history. All of the restaurants and bars have names that hearken back to its historic past – for example, the Tiffin Room or the Billiards Room.

Indeed, there is a legend that the last tiger in Singapore was shot under the billiard table at Raffles. Such romantic (though not for the tiger) tales are part and parcel of Raffles' past. Incidentally, the reality is not nearly so romantic, but is perhaps more fascinating. A tiger escaped from a circus and was cornered underneath the room where the billiard table now stands, which was on stilts at the time, so technically speaking the legend is absolutely correct, if rather stretched. The truth, however, matters little because what people are buying is the Raffles experience and in this respect the legend fits much better!

THINK POINT

Are there any legends or tales from the past in your organization that could be exploited commercially?

Myths and rituals are an important part of what Johnson and Scholes (1984) call the 'cultural web' and are one of the factors that can enhance the perception of an organization, by both the external customer and those who work within the organization and who may be internal customers. It does not matter about the Raffles' tiger; the story itself gives an idea of the type of hotel Raffles is and the past clientele etc.

Afternoon tea or curry tiffin in the Tiffin Room are experiences rather than meals. The food is a mixture of cuisines, representing both local Singapore food and the British past. So, at teatime scones with strawberries and cream or chicken pies will be offered at the same time as local delicacies. The chef who produces the curry tiffin came to Raffles from one of the top hotels in India.

The attention to excellence and detail is well illustrated at tea, when each customer is served an individual pot of the tea of their choice (there is a large range to choose from) by a waiter wearing white gloves. Each pot contains one cup, and as soon as it is finished a new pot is immediately offered. Tea is, therefore, always fresh and never allowed to stew. Waiters watch attentively and customers never need to ask. When they are ready for more tea, it will be there for them!

HOWLER

In a top class hotel in Tahiti, a guest and his wife ordered coffees after an excellent lunch. When the coffee arrived it was stone cold! They called the head waiter over and quietly asked if the coffees could be replaced. The head waiter apologised profusely and promised to send two fresh coffees over straight away. He left the table and went over to the waiter concerned, obviously asking him to take over two replacement coffees.

The waiter arrived at the table holding two new coffees and put them down in front of the guests. He leaned over to the husband and whispered rather bitterly in his ear, 'Of course if you didn't put milk in it, it wouldn't go cold!'

It is well known in the world of marketing that you can sell most things to people once; the crucial question is whether you can sell it to them again. Most organizations are looking for repeat business and Raffles is no exception here. What is remarkable, however, is the fact that the hotel takes such pains to give memorable experiences to many people who cannot afford its core product (overnight stays) and who are possibly only ever going to come once anyway while passing through Singapore. Many organizations in this situation would not go to such trouble. Again, this reflects the aura and atmosphere that Raffles seeks successfully to maintain.

Raffles is owned by DBS Land, which also owns other Great Historic Hotels in the Far East, such as the Royal Hotel in Phnom Penh, Cambodia and the Galle Face in Colombo, Sri Lanka.

Interestingly, when asked who he sees as the main competitors to Raffles, Mr Ng points to famous de luxe hotels such as the Peninsula Hotel in Hong Kong, where afternoon tea is accompanied by live classical music, and the Oriental in Bangkok rather than any local Singapore hotels, many of which he admits are top class.

This shows a truly global outlook, in which customers are choosing the hotel first and the location second. Accordingly, Raffles is marketed globally too.

THINK POINT

Who are your competitors? Can you identify any organizations that are in a similar business to you but which you would not consider to be competitors? List the reasons why.

Although it is a de luxe hotel, Raffles' customers range from backpackers who just want to see it or to drink a Singapore Sling in the famous long bar, where the floor is strewn with peanut shells which crunch as you walk on them, to major personalities and wealthy clients who can afford to stay in the hotel.

Although many business people do stay at the hotel, they are usually doing it as part of their leisure time and, according to Mr Ng, it is usually the customer rather than the company who is paying. The mix of nationalities among customers is quite varied too. About 25 per cent come from Japan, 25 per cent from the USA, 20 per cent from Europe and the remainder from all over the world. Raffles has a deliberate policy of trying to retain this cultural mix among its customers, and has resisted the temptation of targeting specific countries where high incomes prevail.

Some 10 000 people per day pass through the hotel!

Raffles must show excellence throughout the whole range. This is reflected in the staff employed by the hotel, both in quantity and quality.

The hotel has some 104 suites and employs around 800 staff. The fact that many more people use the facilities than actually stay in the suites goes some way to explaining the high staff to customer ratio. However, it still represents a very high concern for the welfare of all Raffles' customers.

In addition to their on-the-job training, the staff are all given two half days' induction training, irrespective of the job they are doing or whether they actually come face to face with customers. One session covers the strand 'Great Historic Hotel' (background), the other 'Delighting patrons with many memorable experiences' (customer service).

In addition, there are management trainee and graduate trainee programmes lasting for a full year, which prepare people for the managerial positions. Training at all levels is seen as an investment in the present and the future. As you would expect, Raffles acts as a magnet for quality staff, who want to be part of the Raffles atmosphere. Many find it very difficult even when they have shone in previous jobs and been specially rewarded for putting themselves out on behalf of customers. Everyone is expected to shine at Raffles. 'Our guests *expect* the extra mile,' says Mr Ng.

THINK POINT

When did you last go the extra mile for a customer?

Staff turnover is very low, at about 5 per cent, roughly half the local industry norm. Singapore has relatively full employment, however, and there is always the danger of losing very highly trained staff to local hotels. However, the glamour of working at Raffles will always be an attraction for employees.

Behind the aura and historic atmosphere, and the apparent hearkening to a bygone era, lies some very high technology coupled with a senior management that is fully up to date with current managerial and strategic thinking.

For example, it provides an excellent example of quality circles at work. Currently, there are five Service Focus Groups (SFGs), which are cross-functional in that each is made up from members of different departments. This means that the impact of any decisions made can be seen from every perspective within the organization. They meet every week to try to identify potential problems and to solve current ones. These SFGs are driven by a steering committee of senior managers; it is expected that there will be some twenty SFGs by the end of 1996.

Raffles shows all the essential ingredients of a Total Quality Management (TQM) system, the essential features of such a system being:

- The use of quality ingredients and components
- High design quality, as you would expect in a de luxe product
- An emphasis on staff training
- A commitment to continuous improvement
- Attention to detail
- Using quality circles to find solutions

We shall look at each of these later in this chapter. (You can read more about TQM in *Managing Operations* in the *In Charge* series.)

THINK POINT

Does your organization conform to these principles?

We will look in a later chapter at how Raffles uses technology to help to get to know the customers personally.

In the meantime, let's have another quotation from Mr Ng:

'We don't just follow the norms; we are the pacesetters.'

EXCELLENCE

Whatever you do, you need to do it well. A concern for excellence is of prime importance.

THINK POINT

What organizations do you consider excellent? What is it about the way they operate that leads you to your conclusion?

The classic work on excellence is *In Search of Excellence* by Tom Peters and Robert Waterman (1982), who looked at a large number of US organizations that had a reputation for excellent products and services – organizations like IBM, Disney and 3M. They found that there were a series of attributes that these companies exhibited; they were all dynamic, they became very customer-orientated ('close to the customer'), they gave their people responsibility and backed them when they took risks, they recognized that all productivity comes through people, they made sure that all of their employees understood the values and mission of the organization. As organizations, they stayed close to what they were good at and didn't try to branch out into unrelated areas; they had simple organizational structures; and they kept a close control on values and costs but allowed employees freedom of action within these constraints. Most of these attributes related directly back to the people who worked for (and, in these days of partnerships, closely with) the organization.

One thing that Peters and Waterman postulated was that in excellent organizations, the employees believed that their organization was the best in its particular business. This is an idea that, perhaps, needs a degree of modification because it is possible for arrogance to creep in, but remember:

GOLDEN RULE

If you don't believe, how can you expect the customer to?

It is worth looking at the Peters and Waterman attributes in some detail because they have provided much of the foundation for studies of excellence and quality from the 1980s onwards. Their studies concluded that there were eight basic attributes of excellent companies backed up by seven basic beliefs. The basic, underlying beliefs of the excellent organizations studied were:

- a belief in being the best
- a belief in the importance of getting the details right
- a belief that the people who worked for the organization were at the heart of its success
- a belief in superior quality and service
- a belief in encouraging innovation and tolerating failure where this was a genuine effort to move the organization on
- a belief in the importance of internal communications
- a belief in the need for the organization to grow economically

Armed with these beliefs, the organizations demonstrated the following eight attributes:

- bias for action
- closeness to the customer
- autonomy and entrepreneurship
- productivity through people
- hands on, value driven
- stick to the knitting
- single form, lean staff
- simultaneous loose–tight properties

Bias for action

The organizations were ones that were innovative and were willing to try things. This attitude is demonstrated by the organizations considered in this book. They are *proactive* rather than *reactive*. Proactivity is about anticipation and making things happen rather than reacting to others all of the time. Much of the success of British Airways has come from the proactive nature of the organization, including the introduction of arrivals lounges and one of the most modern fleets in the air. Tesco, the UK supermarket giant, has pioneered the out-of-town supermarket with large car parks, disabled access and baby facilities. This is a proactive approach to the increase in car ownership.

Closeness to the customer

It is only by talking to customers that you can find out what they want. Michael Boyd is a part-time barman at the Lexington Hotel in Midtown Manhattan. (He is also an accomplished artist and teacher.) Some customers are regulars, others are there for just one or two nights. By getting to know the customer through conversation, Michael not only serves drinks but makes his knowledge of the city and his extensive understanding of US history and institutions available to his customers. He is the quintessential New York barman. He has an uncanny memory for faces and can remember not only favourite drinks but occupations, hobbies etc. By being willing to talk, and, most importantly, listen, Michael and those like him make a drink for travellers a long way from home far more pleasurable than it might be in a strange place.

The staff on the Princess Cruise boats make a point of talking to passengers as they move about the ship. Tom Peters has coined the phrase 'management by wandering around' (MBWA) and stresses the importance of talking to your customers, not just for a hard sell but to find out about their wants and needs. BA has staff in the baggage hall at Heathrow's Terminal 4 who ask arriving passengers about their experience on the journey; Virgin, as we shall see later, has systems for communicating customer comments throughout the organization. It isn't enough for *you* to know what the customer requires and feels; systems need to be in place to communicate the information throughout the organization. Communication with the customer needs to be in the language of the customer, and not jargon. Jargon and technical 'speak' may sound clever and knowledgeable but if the customer cannot understand you or feels that you are being patronizing, he or she may well go elsewhere.

GOLDEN RULE

You must listen to your customers to find out what they want.

THINK POINT

How close are you to your customers? Do you speak their language or expect them to speak yours?

Autonomy and entrepreneurship

Excellent organizations encourage people to take responsibility for decisions within corporate guidelines and in accordance with the mission and vision of the organization. As we shall see in Chapter 7, if you have an idea, such organizations would encourage you. Billy Hygate on the *Royal Princess* was able to alter the running order of entertainments to suit passenger needs. It would be unwise to allow people total freedom, but they need to be allowed the flexibility to respond to the customer. One spin-off is that this is a good motivator of staff.

Productivity through people

One key characteristic of an excellent organization is that it realizes the contribution of all of its staff. This means celebrating success throughout the organization. Ensure that internal customers know what is happening and share in good external customer comments. All quality ultimately depends on the people in the organization. There can be as many quality systems as you like, but without well-motivated, well-informed staff, customer service will suffer.

HOWLER

A UK company had achieved a number of quality awards in the past and was noted for its cutting-edge products and after-sales service. Unfortunately, management changes brought in a regime that put less emphasis on staff morale and development. Soon service levels began to decline and product quality dropped. Despite advertising that stressed the quality standards achieved in the past, sales began to decline. New, tougher systems were implemented but the root cause, staff morale, was never tackled. As sales declined, so staff were laid off and morale declined further – a familiar and depressing spiral had developed that eventually led to a takeover.

If the organization doesn't look after its people, they won't be able to look after the customer.

Hands on, value driven

In excellent organizations, the core values and beliefs of the organization are known and understood by all of the staff. It doesn't matter whether it is a huge multinational like BA, a regional leader like Raffles or a small organization like Cole's Bookstore (see later in this chapter), everybody who works for the organization needs to understand its philosophy and communicate that to the customer. Values are not just something for the boardroom; they are for the hands-on staff as well. Later in this book you will be introduced to the concept of 'organizational body language' – the image that the organization presents to its customers. This must link to the basic philosophy of the organization.

THINK POINT

How conversant are you with the philosophy, mission and vision of your organization?

HOWLER

A car service centre. Above the reception counter is a sign saying:

We are here to serve you.

Ten minutes later and, despite ringing the bell provided, the customer still hasn't been served.

Stick to the knitting

P&O is good at shipping-related activities, Raffles runs a good hotel, Bill Shepard sells books. One thing that Peters and Waterman found was that, although there may be gaps in unrelated markets, organizations were most successful when they stuck to what they were good at. This does not mean that there should not be diversification, but it does need to be planned. P&O is involved in building but under the Bovis name. You may not have any say in the activities of your organization but if you are asked to move away from your core activity, make sure you have the necessary skills for the new tasks; request training, if necessary.

Single form, lean staff

Organizations work best with simple structures. Customers, too, understand simple structures. A complex organization often pushes customers from department to department, and the more complex an organization is, the more difficulties are encountered with communications. If you have to set up any structure within your organization, remember KIS (Keep It Simple).

Simultaneous loose–tight properties

Although it sounds complex, this is a very simple concept. Give the staff at the customer interface as much flexibility as possible but keep a close control on the core values (and the finances) of the organization.

A Rolls-Royce is possibly the best car in the world, and in pure terms it is truly excellent. The most highly rated cruise ship in the world in 1994 (according to the Berlitz *Guide to Cruising and Cruise Ships*, 1994) was Royal Viking Line's *Royal Viking Sun*, but how many people can own a Rolls-Royce or travel on one or two ships (in 1994, Royal Viking Line operated two vessels). If the *Royal Viking Sun* and the other vessel, the *Royal Viking Queen* (the Royal Viking operation was acquired by Cunard in 1995), were full to capacity for 52 weeks of the year – allowing, therefore, for 52 seven-day cruises – only 53 000 people would be able to enjoy the experience – and no ship will be in operation for 365 days per year, without time out for maintenance. Rolls-Royce and

Royal Viking Line are undeniably excellent – they are probably the best in the world – but for most of us, excellence is connected with things that we *can* do or experience.

Marks & Spencer and Tesco in the UK and Macy's in the USA may not be in the same league as very expensive stores but they offer an excellent service to a large number of customers. Ford Motors may not be perceived to be in the same class as Rolls-Royce but it provides good, reliable transportation for millions of people across the world. British Airways operates one of the largest route networks in the world and at prices that a large number of people can afford, and it does it to a consistently high level of service. Princess Cruise, operating all of its vessels over a full 52-week period on a mixture of 7–21 day cruises, could carry approximately 400 000 passengers in a year. To do that with a consistently high service and at prices that are described as 'moderate' in the Berlitz guide is, for most of us, a truer example of excellence.

Excellence as we would want to present it in this book is a balance between the best service or product for the price and the highest quality, delivered to a consistently high level. All this is done through people. Excellence is the equilibrium between the various components (figure 11). (If a conscious decision has been made to go for a small 'niche' market, then one cannot compare the products or services so developed with those that are aimed at a wider market. When considering excellence it is important that like is compared with like.)

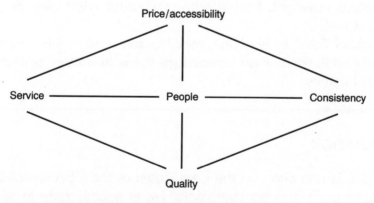

Figure 11 The excellence equilibrium

SERVICE

Remember that you have internal as well as external customers. Everybody whom you relate to is a customer in the widest sense of the word.

Service is about taking responsibility – going the extra mile, as Raffles does. Customers make mistakes but the essence of good service is when you take responsibility for the problem. You may need to advise them as to what they need to do, and there will be things that only they can do: you cannot sign forms for them but you can show them that they have a 'friend' within the organization. We all have a fair idea of what is acceptable; excellence is when you go that extra mile, when you do more than they might have expected. If they are angry or upset, you may not receive any thanks but they and, more importantly, you will know that you did all that you possibly could. There is an important role for the organization here. Unless the organizational competencies are present, then the motivation to exercise personal competence will be missing. Smile, even if it is a bad day – it shows that you care.

CONSISTENCY

Everybody is entitled to consistency of service or product for the price they have paid. They are entitled to acceptability, whatever they have paid. You may not like all of your customers, whether internal or external, but if you are concerned about delivering personal excellence, they will all be treated to the same high, consistent standard. People who care about what they do, tend to do it well.

Michael Boyd in his New York bar treats all of his customers equally well; there is no favouritism there, and there is plenty of repeat business.

PARADOX

There is one shop on the East Coast of the USA where the owner is rude to his customers. He is equally rude to all of them, thus fulfilling our consistency requirement, and his prices are the cheapest in the county. One shop can probably get away with this. It becomes an experience to shop there and be subjected to mild abuse. It works, but it is a paradox and not a customer service concept we recommend.

QUALITY

Quality is never delivering second best. Even if you only have a small part to play in a service or product, play it to your best. Don't cut corners – it only leads to more work. Take a pride in what you do. Even if you feel that it is a humble role, never provide second best. Think about how you can improve what you do. Others will notice and their performance will improve. Don't tell people how high your standards are (that's a sure way to make enemies): show them by quiet, consistent examples, and then let them tell you (and their friends!).

Things will go wrong. What do you do to recover the situation? British Airways ran a training programme for all of their staff worldwide in 1993/94, called 'Winning for Customers'; it focused on those things that the ordinary member of the airline could do to assist the customer, and how to take responsibility and recover when things, as they do, went wrong: when baggage went astray, when connections were lost, when special requirements were needed. Such an organizational competence needs to be matched by a commitment to personal competence, and only you can make that commitment. Chapter 5 will look at recovering when things go wrong.

PRICE/ACCESSIBILITY

You may not control price but you need to understand it. There is a balance between the price somebody is prepared to pay and the price you are prepared to deliver for. Weight it on their side. People are reasonable; they don't want the earth, but they do want value for money (or time). The following organizations, which are just a few examples amongst many, all deliver value for money: British Airways, Tesco, Raffles, Cole's Bookshop, The Red Caboose, Rover and Princess Cruises. Their service seems better than you would have expected at the price. A British Telecom manager who travelled 40 miles to deliver a fax machine to replace a faulty one in order to save the customer a journey; the person on the street who takes you to a place that is hard to find, rather than just giving you instructions: these are examples of excellence and, again, they are related to people.

A key point about value for money in particular, and excellence in general, is that talking somebody into something they cannot afford may make you a short-term profit, but you are unlikely to see that person again. If you give a value-for-money product at a price people can afford, they will come back, and repeat business is a key organizational performance indicator.

THINK POINT

Does your organization have repeat business as a key performance indicator? Is it actually measured?

Accessibility is linked to price. As we have stated, like must be compared with like. A lower priced product or service is likely to be more accessible. Organizations often have two choices: low volume/high margin (Rolls-Royce) or high volume/low margin (Ford) – they cater for very different markets and each may be considered excellent in its own way.

If there is an overriding factor, it is quality, and as disposable incomes increase, so does the demand for quality. There is an anecdotal story about a couple in the former communist bloc of Eastern Europe. They actually purchased a non-working washing machine, because a non-working machine was better than none at all. Such a concept would seem alien to more consumer-orientated eyes; your customers not only want the product or service, they want a product or service that actually delivers its intended function. Indeed, in both the USA and Europe, products must deliver as intended or else the supplier is in breach of consumer legislation.

However, quality is not solely about products or people, as Edgar Wille (1992) has pointed out:

The total quality approach is about people and attitudes. It's not about techniques and procedures as such. It includes them, and it needs them. However, it's the people who actually use them, inspired with a simple idea that the purpose of work is to provide customers with something that will delight them and make them want to keep paying your salary, by buying the product or service that you provide.

Wille's book is worth reading in its entirety in order to understand how the concepts of quality have been brought about and to gain an insight into the thinking of the 'quality' gurus: Deming, Juran, Crosby etc.

Probably the best known of these is W. Edward Deming, who was involved with the rebuilding of Japanese industry after its devastation in 1945. Deming realized that the pursuit of quality depended on a highly trained, motivated and empowered work-force, and that constant inspections linked to fear and a plethora of slogans did not help the achievement of quality.

One phrase that Wille uses, and which may seem strange, is to 'delight the customer' but in essence this is what quality is – it is delighting the customer; it is giving the customer, whether internal or external, more than he or she expected at the same or lower cost. It may be hard to determine analytically when delight has occurred but you can see it in the customer's eyes and atti-tude: you know it when it is there. Delight is far, far more than merely satisfying!

THINK POINT

When and how did you last truly delight a customer?

The 1990s have seen the growth of megastores, not just for food and clothes, but for records/CDs, computers and software, holidays and even books. The small bookseller has had a lean time competing with those who can carry larger stocks, even when protected by industry pricing policies such as the Net Book Agreement in the UK. One shop that has proved successful by delighting the customer is Cole's Bookshop in Bicester (pronounced 'Bister') in the UK. Bill Shepard, the owner, has a clearly defined strategy for attracting and retaining his customer base. First, it is a bookshop where all are welcome. Despite its small size, it is laid out in a welcoming manner and there is even a play area for children. Book buying is a 'browsing' experience, thus somewhere for the children to play enables customers to consider volumes at a more leisurely pace. The staff, including Bill, are knowledgeable about books and enthuse about them. They know who wrote what and who writes similar books. People often come in and say that they have enjoyed something and would like another book on the same theme or in the same style. Staff knowledge enables this customer need to be met.

The staff make time to search the computer database and have links with specialist suppliers who can trace out-of-print volumes at reasonable cost.

Cole's Bookshop's latest *unique selling point* (USP) is the supply of signed editions at no extra cost. Bill acquires copies of new books and has them signed by the author, thus allowing purchasers that something different and a possible future investment.

Interestingly, Bill moved into book selling from the cut-throat world of 'brown goods' (hi fi, TVs and videos cassette recorders) retailing and is only too well aware that books, like the latter products, can suffer a decline in sales in a recession unless the retailer goes the extra mile. One of his overriding philosophies is that if you make a promise you must deliver – would that all suppliers had that creed.

HOWLER

'Yes sir, we'll deliver it on Wednesday.'
So the customer of this major domestic retailer arranges to stay home for the day.
They did deliver on Wednesday, but it wasn't the right product – do you think they received repeat business?

Jill Galt, the singer mentioned in chapter 1, has to 'delight' her audience. An excellent performer must do more than know the words and hit the right notes; he or she must add something to the score and the lyrics to make the experience special. Successful performers add something of themselves to the basic 'product', and all those dealing with customers, whether they be internal or external, can add value, i.e. move from the basic towards excellence.

QUALITY CIRCLES

The Unipart Group of Companies (UGC) in the UK is involved in the manufacture and distribution of car components. To ensure that it has a suitably trained workforce, it set up its own university, the Unipart 'U', which, among other things, teaches team problem-solving techniques used in quality circles, together with a large number of quality circles. *Quality circles* were first conceived by Karo Ishikawa and Jeff Beardsley in the 1970s as workgroup-based improvement forums, where those who are closest to the task or problem under consideration meet to consider solutions and improvements. They became very popular in Japan and their introduction has spread to the rest of the world. By giving ownership to those at the sharp end, rather than management dictating solutions, they have motivated staff towards quality approaches. Coupled with the idea that every member of the workforce should be responsible for his or her quality control, a concept that helped to revitalize Rover cars, they are a useful ingredient in a quality system.

The Unipart quality circles are known as OCC (Our Contribution Counts) circles, and their achievements are celebrated through special events called 'Closing Ceremonies', at which executives present special certificates, which are displayed throughout Unipart locations

---

THINK POINT

How do you and your organization 'celebrate' the achievement of quality and excellence?

Too many managers punish mistakes but fail to celebrate successes. As Peters and Waterman have shown, successful companies make a point of celebrating success; it is a wonderful motivator!

By involving staff, suppliers and customers in the pursuit of quality, not just in terms of the actual product but in the way that training and staff development are carried out, companies like Unipart have produced a 'seamless quality web' that gives ownership and benefits to all concerned with the organization.

The National Railroad Passenger Corporation (otherwise known as AMTRAK), the intercity passenger rail operator in the USA, is not a name synonymous with quality, yet AMTRAK is trying hard to raise its standards and is achieving a great deal of success.

As mentioned in the previous chapter, the US railroads had great difficulty from the 1960s in competing with the growth in car ownership and the development of relatively inexpensive and extremely fast inter-continental air travel. The great names of American railroading – the Union Pacific, Atchison, Topeka and Santa Fe, Baltimore and Ohio, Pennsylvania and the New York Central – could no longer afford to operate passenger trains against competition from each other and the airlines. The latter two merged in 1968 (legal disputes delaying the actual merger from its agreement in 1961) to form the Penn Central Railroad, but the writing was on the wall and Penn Central entered bankruptcy proceedings in 1970 following a loss of nearly $326m.

As a result of the collapse of Penn Central and the ailing fortunes of the other rail carriers, AMTRAK was formed to take over long-distance passenger rail services in the USA, freeing the railroads to concentrate on freight operations. Penn Central was rescued via the Rail Revitalization and Reform Act in 1973 and its assets were taken over by the Consolidated Rail Corporation, or CONRAIL, in 1976.

AMTRAK inherited an old system with a declining customer base that was faced with intense competition from the airlines. A not too dissimilar situation has existed in Europe, but the distances are shorter and the new high speed trains such as the French TGV and the German ICE are able to compete with the airlines on a city centre to city centre basis. Although the flight from London to Paris takes just over an hour, check-in requirements and the travel times from the centres of each city to and from the airport add to this greatly, and the 3.5 hours of the Eurostar train through the Channel Tunnel from London Waterloo Station to Paris Gare du Nord is highly competitive.

One set of routes where these factors apply to AMTRAK is the north-east corridor running from Boston, in Massachusetts, through New York to Washington, DC. The Metroliner service from New York Penn Station to Washington Union Station, a distance of 225 miles, takes 3 hours, a figure comparable to the services of British Rail. Penn Station is in the heart of Manhattan, and one can see the Capitol Building and other historic sites on exit from the beautifully restored Union Station in Washington. The trains are comfortable, although still somewhat below European prestige intercity services, with a goodly amount of leg room and catering facilities. By matching airline-type services, AMTRAK has been able to acquire a 33 per cent market share on this important route.

New York's Penn Station is a shadow of its former self. While the more famous Grand Central Terminus on 42nd Street has been saved, the original McKim building on 32nd Street was razed and redeveloped underground from 1962, a destruction akin to the demolition and rebuilding in a modern functional style of London's Euston Station. The new station can be a daunting experience. The passenger, whichever entrance he or she chooses, must descend into the bowels of New York, to be faced with a huge concourse with side alleys leading to the New York Subway, the PATH trains to New Jersey and the Long Island Rail Road. Faced with concerns about passenger security and comfort (traditionally US railway stations have provided very little seating, both Grand Central and the original Penn Station having no seats in the waiting area, in classic Roman style), AMTRAK decided not only to improve the train service but to look after the comfort and security of its passengers within the station.

To this end, AMTRAK has looked at the needs of customers waiting for trains and provided secure areas for them. Premium passengers – those travelling on first class tickets (AMTRAK's Club Service and first class sleeping car passengers) – are able to use the AMTRAK Metropolitan Lounges situated at Penn Station, Philadelphia, Chicago and Washington, DC. These airline-style lounges feature a complimentary soft drinks service, newspapers and magazines, television, telephones and washrooms, and provide a peaceful area to wait for the train or to catch up on work. The Metroliner service is well suited to the business traveller, with a departure to and from Washington approximately every hour. Additional and upgraded parking has been provided at Trenton NJ, Metropark NJ and Baltimore MD, such parking being of especial interest to the business traveller.

> **GOLDEN RULE**
>
> In a free market economy, never forget that the customer has a choice.

Anyone wishing to travel from New York to Washington, DC can drive, take a bus, catch a plane or use AMTRAK. To ensure maximum uptake, AMTRAK needs to add more value for money than the competition. The whole ambience of the Metropolitan Lounges is that of tranquillity and safety, including an atmosphere not polluted by tobacco smoke – like many of the eastern corridor trains and all US internal flights, the lounges have a strict no smoking rule – and the staff are well trained to look after the needs of premium customers. By providing a relaxed and welcoming atmosphere, Sandy Randolph, one of the Penn Station Metropolitan Lounge receptionists in 1995, believes that it is possible to bring on side those whose day has started badly. A trip to the station through the New York rush hour can be very tiring and she sees the lounge as the place where the relaxing train trip starts. The lounge at Penn Station was opened in 1990 and caters for about 200 customers per day. Some of these customers have expressed surprise and initially treated the staff with less respect than one might expect. – 'after all, this is only AMTRAK' – but care in providing customer service has seen repeat business increase over the years and now they are receiving comments of surprise when trains are sold out, as happens.

> **THINK POINT**
>
> What steps does your organization take to look after the safety and security of your customers?

Sandy sees much of her job in terms of the way she relates to customers, e.g. tone of voice, and her knowledge of the AMTRAK system (she joined the railroad in 1977). At times there are difficulties to deal with. Customers without the correct type of ticket allowing lounge access have to be persuaded, politely, to leave without risking losing their future business.

The staff are hand picked and work closely together to ensure consistency. Before being appointed, they have to make a presentation on customer service to senior managers.

AMTRAK's focus on customer service is championed from the highest levels of the organization. Robert Vanderclute, who in 1995 was the acting Chief Executive Officer of AMTRAK Intercity Rail Service, believes that the key to excellence lies with the staff and that 'the people believe in what they are doing'. He acknowledges that AMTRAK has seen hard times but that the staff, having seen the bad times through, can see the company coming back into the market as a strong player. Despite the problems of the past, he believes that the staff are dedicated to AMTRAK. The company is working hard on its CQI (Continuous Quality Improvement) programme, which stresses the needs of both internal and external customers and that success depends on those on the first line, i.e. the sharp end, as we stressed in chapter 1.

Earlier in this chapter, while looking at TQM, we said that a commitment to continuous improvement was an essential ingredient of any TQM system. The staff at the Union Station HQ of AMTRAK in Washington, DC, have that commitment. From Robert Vanderclute downwards, they admit that they are not there yet but they have a vision of where they want the organization to be and, through their CQI programme, a vehicle for getting there.

One of the driving forces behind the Metropolitan Lounge concept was Suzi Andiman, the then Manager of Passenger Handling, who sees the idea in terms of value added, a concept that the airlines which pioneered the lounge concept would understand. In 1994, British Airways went a step beyond the departure lounge concept to set up arrival lounges for premium passengers, with showers etc., at London's Heathrow and Gatwick airports. Suzi describes the lounges as 'an oasis in the maelstrom of activity', but then stresses the human element in that the lounge facilities are nothing without smiling faces! Indeed, she uses the concierge idea as a role model for lounge reception staff. They are there to do more than act as gatekeepers; they are sources of information and assistance. The staff are given ownership of the facility and are encouraged to participate in design and operational issues.

While the lounges cater for the premium passengers, the 'coach' passengers have not been forgotten. Given the intimidating nature of large railway stations the world over – Penn Station is not unique in having homeless people sleeping in its more secluded areas – secure waiting areas with attendants have been set up to provide a safer environment for all who choose to use the train.

Although it is still possible to cross the USA by rail – and the great names are still there: 'the Sunset Limited', 'the Gulf Breeze', 'the Capitol Limited' and 'the Empire Builder' – AMTRAK is looking to new markets, especially the vacation market, as is VIA Rail in Canada. It is not easy. The route network is still shrinking and there needs to be a continuing large investment in new track and rolling stock. The future of rail travel in the USA is likely to be that of high quality, relaxing journeys linking major cities. The north-east corridor presents a good opportunity to provide a high quality, value added service that can compete by looking at what the customer requires and then providing it. Experiences in Europe suggest that there is still a market for high quality intercity services, and, given the enthusiasm and commitment to quality of the AMTRAK management and staff, they seem well placed to consolidate and increase their market share.

British Airways, which is a very customer driven organization and one of the few profitable airlines in the world, has made excellence one of its bywords.

Operating, together with their partners, the largest route network in the world, consistency and quality are all important. 'Winning for Customers', a massive two-year worldwide training programme, has already been mentioned in this chapter. BA also runs a 'Certificate in Management Studies' and a 'Fundamentals in Customer Service' programme for staff, again on a worldwide basis. This emphasis on staff training is another of the key features of a TQM system.

THINK POINT

How much training do you and your colleagues receive on customer satisfaction, quality and associated topics? Is it sufficient?

One point that BA stresses is that there is a tradeoff between customer care and costs. Organizations must control their costs. All excellent organizations care about costs: they would go out of business if they didn't. Given an infinite pot of money, it should be possible to have the most flawless service possible. What organizations need to aim for, however, is the highest possible service within the cost constraints. The whole concept of value for money is about the balance between what is provided and what it costs. Customers want the best service possible but not at a price that puts the product or service beyond their reach. This is the point of having quality and accessibility in the excellence equilibrium (figure 11).

The other features of a TQM system need consideration. Quality demands the best possible resources, be they raw materials, manufactured ingredients or the human resource. The world's major automobile manufacturers now work closely with their major suppliers to ensure that the components coming into the factories are of the highest possible quality. The concept of a zero defect rate is becoming achievable in more and more industries. There is no doubt that standards for supplies have risen over the past few years. In the 1950s and 1960s it was not unusual for the purchaser of a new automobile to have to return it to the dealer a number of times to have faults rectified. Rover is so sure of the quality of its current products that it offers to take a vehicle back within one month or 1000 miles if the customer is not satisfied, even if it is a case of 'buyer's regret', as it is termed in the USA, and there is no fault with the product. Not only has the quality of components risen but so has that of design. Designs of both products and services are much more customer driven. Suppliers need to ask: what does my customer want and how can I deliver it?

The final component of a TQM system is attention to detail:

His lord said unto him, Well done, good and faithful servant; thou hast been faithful over a few things, I will make thee ruler over many things: enter thou into the joy of thy lord. (Matthew 25:23)

Earlier in this chapter we spoke about 'delighting the customer'. It is often the small, perhaps unexpected, things that cause the greatest delight: an automobile dealer placing a bottle of champagne in the boot (trunk) of a new car; a waiter who remembers your favourite drink; a BA stewardess who, seeing a bored child on a long-haul flight, arranges for her to visit the flight deck. Equally, some of the more voracious complaints are not about major problems, but small niggles. By ensuring that you attend to the details, you can be confident about the overall quality of your service or product. As they say in the UK:

Look after the pennies and the pounds will look after themselves.

QUALITY STANDARDS

Whenever you think about quality it should be in terms of SMART criteria. SMART is an acronym that stands for:

Specific
Measurable
Achievable
Realistic
Timely

It is easy to be very subjective about quality, but in order to measure it we need to think objectively, hence the need for SMART criteria.

Examples of quality standards, adapted from *Managing Operations* by Cartwright et al., are:

- QUANTITY: as in the number of matches in a box
- TIME WITHOUT FAILURE: as in the life of an automobile component
- TIME WITHIN WHICH: as in the time within which a letter will be answered
- SIZE: as in the length of a screw or nail
- APPEARANCE: does the new automobile have any blemishes?
- STRENGTH: the stated breaking strain of a component
- KEEPING TO CONTRACT: does the holiday conform exactly to the brochure description?
- ON TIME: are delivery promises met?

All of the above are measurable and realistic: achievable standards can be set. They need to be realistic to avoid the danger of making something to too high a standard. In the early days of the auto-mobile industry, Henry Ford discovered that the kingpins on the Model T could be recovered from scrapped vehicles, with plenty of life left in them. The trouble is, most motorists would not want used kingpins. The originals were over-engineered. The answer was to make the kingpins to a lower, *but still acceptable in terms of life expectancy and safety,* standard, which in turn could cut manufacturing costs.

There are now national and international standards set down for many areas of production and service. There are British Standards, e.g. BS5750 for quality management systems and its equivalent ISO (International Organization for Standardization) 9000, a series of standards for computer keyboards, fire extinguishers and toys, among other consumer goods. Whatever the awarding body, the product or service must conform to all requirements of the standard in order to use the standard mark and thus claim to be a quality product. Care needs to be taken not to become complacent, as mentioned in the LICAL acronym in the previous chapter.

The Royal Mail steamer *Titanic*, which sank early in the morning of 15 April 1912, met every one and exceeded many of the relevant national and international standards for a large seagoing pas-senger vessel. Standards need to evolve, and nothing can take away the need for individual vigilance on quality issues.

HOWLER

A medium-sized company had a standard that said that the telephone must be answered within four rings – very com-mendable, and the standard was met with consistency. Unfortunately, the staff were very poor at dealing with tele-phone enquires, so, although the standard was met, the customers were not satisfied.

CONTROL OF QUALITY

There are statistical techniques, detailed consideration of which is beyond the scope of this book, that allow for conformity to a standard to be measured. This is easier within the manufacturing sector, where many of the quality standards relate to physical or operational characteristics of the product. The use of standard deviation, process and acceptance sampling, Pareto and other analyses can help the organization see how close to its quality measures it is. Every organization, however, can measure quality via customer comments, repeat and new business, and complaints. Complaints are especially important because:

GOLDEN RULE

Welcome complaints; they allow for recovery.

As has been stated earlier, in free-market economies, quality is becoming a very important determinate of purchase choice. BA, Princess Cruises, AMTRAK, Cole's Bookshop and others quoted in this volume are conscious of the need to reach higher and higher quality standards but are also aware that there is no point in doing so if the resultant costs make their product or service uncompetitive or inaccessible.

SUMMARY

This chapter has looked at excellence in terms of quality, accessibility, consistency and service. The work of Tom Peters and Robert Waterman was considered in some detail. It must not be forgotten, however, that the effects on the financial bottom line need to be considered. Quality can be measured, and this should be done using SMART criteria detailed above.

4
Where Everybody Knows Your Name

EFFECTIVE COMMUNICATION

The quotation in the heading for this chapter is taken from the classic American television programme *Cheers*, which centres around a bar in the city of Boston. At the very beginning each week one of the central characters is shown entering the bar, and as he does so every one shouts his name, 'Norm', in greeting.

While it is not expected that every organization should shout out its customers' names at every opportunity, there are very important issues here. Many organizations are finding that customers feel much more comfortable doing business with people who know them, and are sometimes even prepared to pay a little more because of this close relationship.

In this chapter we will look at some organizations that have taken this to heart and have set out to get to know their customers better, in many instances by name. The main organizations that we will look at here are:

- Taj Hotels in Jaipur
- Virgin Airlines
- Home Housing

but we will be mentioning others along the way.

The Taj Group's Rambagh Palace Hotel in Jaipur, India is a magnificent building covering some 47 acres. It was originally a real maharajah's palace, and this is very clear to visitors as they approach through the main entrance. The beautiful gardens and landscape are carefully tended by some 40–50 staff to ensure that it blooms throughout the dust and heat of the long hot Jaipur summer, when it may not rain for several months and temperatures can reach the high forties Celsius.

Arriving in Jaipur itself is often the culmination of a long, hard car or coach journey by many tourists, and the Rambagh Palace provides a quiet, magnificent, luxurious, green oasis where they can relax and enjoy the usual amenities of a de luxe hotel.

It is against this background that the management and staff of the hotel strive to achieve a high degree of customer satisfaction. Indeed, the resident manager, Mr Anil Paranjpe, put the problem very succinctly:

> 'Our aim is to manage *Royally with efficiency.* People want all of the ambience of the former Maharajah's Palace but they also want fax machines, a hot bath and a shower and fine dining in the restaurant.'

The management at the Rambagh believe that the key issue is to know who their customers are and to identify what they want. The hotel has three main target markets:

- Tour operators
- Independent travellers
- Business travellers

The latter markets are very similar and in many respects are intermingled. The recent liberalization of Indian industry has meant that there has been a terrific upsurge in the number of business people travelling to India. Indeed, India is seen by many major companies as the main growth area for business opportunities over the next few years. Most international flights into and from India are flying with a full complement of business and first class passengers, and the luxury hotels in Delhi and Bombay, the international gateways, have whole floors set aside for people who need to work while staying at the hotel.

Many of these clients will visit cities like Jaipur because of a specific business opportunity in which they are interested. Others will extend their business trip to Delhi or Bombay by taking a few days to see the sights, and in effect become independent travellers for the duration of their stay in Jaipur. In many cases, these visitors may be influential people in major companies and offer the Rambagh Palace a great opportunity to impress them and thus gain future business, not only from the particular client but also from his or her organization.

The needs of such clients can be quite different from those who arrive with organized tour operators. Those travelling on tours work to a regimented timetable set out by their tour leader, who will have agreed it with the hotel in advance. Breakfast, lunch and dinner are arranged for set times and baggage is handled with quiet efficiency. A buffet menu is provided, which is often served on a 'help yourself' basis. There is a choice of cuisine covering continental, Chinese and Indian, reflecting the many different nationalities of the guests and ensuring that there will always be a choice for them, whichever style they prefer.

One thing that is common to all of the market segments, however, is that, whether travelling independently or in a group, they still expect the hotel to treat them individually and to respond to their individual needs. They are, after all, in a palace and expect to be treated as an honoured guest.

To this end, the Taj Group take an ancient Sanskrit saying to heart and proudly claim that in Taj Hotels, 'The guest is God'.

It is no accident that such fundamental beliefs, which were the code by which people lived in the great civilizations of the past, should underpin so much of marketing theory in the 1990s, where we now say, 'The customer is King'.

The Rambagh Palace has some 270 employees, of whom 40–50 work in the gardens. Several others are employed to sweep away the Jaipur dust from the vast expanses of corridors that run through the hotel. There are 106 rooms and, assuming full double occupancy and allowing for the sweepers and gardeners, this still leaves an almost one to one ratio between hotel guests and actual hotel staff.

The result is that there is always someone available to assist a guest with a heavy suitcase, or to help someone choose from the dinner menu or to recommend one of the cocktails at the bar.

Every single one of the 106 rooms at the Rambagh Palace is different from all of the others. Standard rooms are large, while many of the superior rooms and suites carry names that appeal to the status needs of the guests who reserve them. It also helps them to identify with a particular room, which they may particularly enjoy.

In this respect, the Taj Group is currently introducing a very powerful piece of technology, which is likely to give them a significant competitive edge. Fidelio has already been installed in the Taj Group hotels in Delhi and Bombay and will soon be operating throughout the whole group. Essentially, it is a network of computers that allows a database of customer details and preferences to be maintained, updated and accessed by all of the hotels on the system.

This means that a client who likes a particular type of room can have one allocated when the reservation is made. Requirements for facilities such as laptop computers or fax machines, or even for a particular type of fruit in the room's fruit bowl, can also be fed into the database. As any Taj hotel can update the information, new preferences as they emerge can be input and then accessed by all other hotels.

HOWLER

On arrival at a British airport, a couple waited for a coach to take them to their home, roughly an hour and a half's journey from the airport. They had flown in from Los Angeles that morning after an eleven-hour flight, which itself had been preceded by a three-hour coach journey to Los Angeles airport. Add the two-hour check-in period, and they had been travelling for some sixteen hours.

The coach arrived and stopped. The driver got out and opened the luggage compartment on the side of the coach. The man pulled the suitcase to the side of the bus. Other passengers did the same. The driver looked at them in some amusement. 'Don't you want your luggage to go with you then? Suit yourselves.'

At this, the passengers understood that they were expected to load their own cases into the bus, which they all did, including two American visitors who were clearly incredulous.

The first to load their case as they were first in the queue, the couple walked to the door of the bus and began to climb up the short stairway.

Suddenly a shout of, 'Get off that bus now!' could be heard

resounding around the front of the airport. The couple froze and turned round in astonishment.

'Can't you read?' said the driver, with a sneer.

'Not very well at the moment,' replied the man, 'as I've been travelling now for over sixteen hours and my concentration is not what it was' – which, of course, is why he had arranged to use a bus rather than drive his own car.

'Well, there's a notice on the window which says that passengers are not allowed to enter when there is no driver on the bus, so get off now!'

'Wow!' said one of the Americans, 'Welcome home!'

Raffles Hotel in Singapore also uses a database to ensure that staff know as much as they can about their customers and their preferences. Photographs of clients are even kept on the database, so that when a member of staff is sent to meet the guest at the airport, he or she can proactively identify the guest rather than stand with a name card, inviting the guest to make him or herself known.

In addition, guests have a personal valet, who can be summoned by a bell. Response time to this bell is monitored by management.

These are both examples of what Mr Ng, whom we met earlier, refers to as the 'understated' service provided by Raffles in that 'You can feel it but you can't see it'.

HOWLER

A guest flew into Darwin in Australia from Britain, arriving at his hotel at nearly four o'clock in the morning. Because he was arriving in the middle of the night, he had to pay for accommodation for the previous night and he had paid in advance through his travel agent. When he arrived, he found that, despite paying in advance, his room had been allocated to someone else and he had to be transferred to another hotel.

It may seem difficult to try to get to know people when you

have millions of customers all over the world. However, hi tech databases do offer opportunities here. Many airlines now have frequent flier programmes, which have two main aims. The first is to lock the customer into a loyal relationship with the airline. The other is to gain as much knowledge about their customers' preferences as possible.

Supermarkets have introduced similar cards for similar reasons.

GOLDEN RULE

It costs far more to gain a new customer than to retain an existing one.

GOOD EXAMPLE

A couple arrive at the reception desk to check in at the Mandarin Hotel in Singapore. It is about half past eight in the evening. They have been travelling from the UK on a thirteen-hour flight and are looking rather dishevelled. The duty manager comes over to introduce herself and wishes them a pleasant stay. They thank her and go off to their room.

Next evening, the couple are going out to dinner and are looking transformed after a night's sleep. As they cross the lobby, the duty manager comes over and addresses them by name and compliments the lady on the lovely dress that she is wearing. The hotel has hundreds of rooms and most of them are occupied!

The management of the Taj Rambagh Palace have already identified a number of changes that they need to make in response to the changing needs of their customers. For example, they have recently increased the opening hours of the coffee shop and bar. They used to be open only when the tours were expected to be in residence at the hotel. However, independent and business travellers are likely to arrive or depart at any time of the day and have much less regimented meal times.

Similarly, new technology is being introduced for the use of guests. Even those business clients who are taking in a few days' sightseeing may need to have frequent contact with their colleagues in Delhi or Bombay or with their organization in their home country, while for those checking out business opportunities such facilities are essential. So the hotel will be making available fax machines and laptop computers with networking capabilities for clients in their rooms, as well as offering a business centre in the hotel.

Another area where the Taj Group has realized from customer feedback that improvements need to be made is in the swimming pool. It is an indoor pool, which is currently unheated and is therefore rather cold. In the Indian winter it is very cold and is little used. The same applies to the pool at the Taj Palace in Delhi, which becomes very cold during the evening in winter. As the Indian winter is the peak period for overseas visitors, there is clearly a need to heat the pools. Already a new solar heated pool, a very efficient method of heating in this part of the world, has been installed at the Taj Jai Mahal Palace Hotel, also in Jaipur, and its success will now be repeated in the Rambagh Palace in the near future.

People are very important to the Taj Group, and for this reason the group has a policy of offering training to all of the staff it employs. This ranges from simple induction and orientation for staff who will not be in regular close contact with the client, such as gardeners, but who do need to be able to respond to guests who are asking directions or want to seek some kind of assistance. So all staff are aware of where everything is in the hotel and who is responsible for what.

Staff who are working in areas where they are directly interacting with the guests spend time in every department of the hotel so that they can understand how they all work. This allows them to decide where they would most like to work, but also shows them how all of the various aspects of the hotel play their own vital part in producing the final overall effect for the customer's comfort and convenience. Depending upon the particular job, induction may last for between two weeks and a month.

In addition, during the low season staff may interchange between hotels. Supervisory staff in Delhi may be assigned to Jaipur for a season in order to get to know the different problems that confront different hotels and to learn how to deal with them.

As Mr Paranjpe says, 'It increases their experience and broadens their outlook. We see it as very important to develop our supervisors and managers'. Staff from the Rambagh Palace may also go for a spell to Delhi or Bombay. The group training policy is coordinated from the Human Resources Department in Bombay and is standard throughout the whole group. Managerial training is also given in the form of workshops aimed at developing the skills of managers in areas such as team building, motivation and customer focus.

Equally important, according to Mr Paranjpe, the resident manager, is the fact that marketing staff who are based in Bombay are able to spend time at all of the hotels throughout the group, thus allowing them to get to know what is available in each hotel and in each geographical area, such as what excursions are available, what type of cuisine, or what types of shops or crafts prevail. This ensures that the marketing people only market what they know the group can deliver in any particular location.

As with the rooms at the Rambagh Palace, each of the Taj hotels is different. Each has its own distinct style. Yet, for all of the differences, there is a standardization of approach aimed at ensuring the absolute comfort of the guest. From the first hotel to be built, which was the Taj Mahal at Bombay in 1933, the group has grown to include many hotels in several countries. As the company motto says, they strive to be 'India's first, Asia's finest!'

Let's now look at Virgin Atlantic Airlines. To anyone who is interested in travel or going on holiday, the name Virgin Atlantic usually conjures up an image of the chairman, Richard Branson. He is a good communicator and is a very high profile personality. Because of this high profile, most people think that Virgin is a much bigger airline than it actually is, largely due to the excellent public relations efforts to ensure that the company remains in the public eye.

In this respect, the chairman is very important. When he travels on company aeroplanes he takes a notebook with him and will make a note of any problems encountered by individual passengers. He has an image in which people see him as being very innovative and very much in touch with ordinary people, reflected in the major drive that the airline has undertaken to improve services in the economy cabin, by introducing individual seat back videos and recently enhancing this facility with interactive video games.

He is also known to have a sense of humour, revealed in publicity material available from the Virgin Public Relations office by the anecdote that when, early in the development of the airline, it was decided that only two classes of travel would be offered, Business Class and Economy, he suggested that they be called Upper Class and Riff Raff! However, wiser counsels prevailed.

The company currently has thirteen aircraft, with three on order, all individually named, currently working over ten routes, although additional routes are worked in conjunction with partner airlines, and five new major destinations are planned.

As mentioned above, Virgin Atlantic offer choices:

- UPPER CLASS (the airline Business Class)
- ECONOMY CLASS, which is segmented into Premium Economy Class (a full fare separate economy cabin) and Economy (all other economy fares)

There is an interesting example here of how Virgin listens to its customers. The Premium Economy used to be called Mid Class, and Virgin received a lot of feedback from customers who expected it to correspond to other airlines' Business Class rather than being an enhanced economy. This led to some dissatisfaction, so the product was renamed to ensure that there could be no misunderstanding. It is now proving very popular.

How this feedback was picked up by the company demonstrates even more the commitment of Virgin to communicating with its customers.

There is a Virgin Top Ten list of issues that is compiled every month and sent to the Directors. It contains the ten issues most commented (criticism or praise) upon by customers by telephone, feedback forms on aircraft and by written complaint. Barbara Garwood, Senior Executive in Customer Relations, sees this Top Ten list as a major force for change. It is taken very seriously, and the Mid Class issue was identified and rectified as a direct result of this.

Barbara says that the number one issue at the moment concerns smoking on aeroplanes. Due to customer demand, Virgin Atlantic took the decision on 8 May 1995 to become 'non-smoking' on all routes except Tokyo and Athens, on which there is still a significant demand for smoking.

> **GOLDEN RULE**
>
> You must listen to your customers to find out what they want.

> **HOWLER**
>
> A conversation in a baker's shop in the heart of England.
> 'Four bread rolls please.'
> 'It's cheaper if you have five.'
> 'But I only need four.'
> 'Four will cost you 88p but five will cost you only 85p.'
> 'Can't you just charge me 85p and only give me four and then you can resell the fifth and make a profit?'
> 'Sorry, if you only have four it'll cost you 88p.'
> 'Five rolls then, I suppose.'
> '85p please.'

In her job, Barbara has a very high degree of involvement with customers. She sees regular contact with customers as very important. In many airlines this would mean the First or Business Class customers only but Barbara has some interesting stories to tell of economy passengers whom she has got to know really well. She points particularly to those people who require just that little bit more – the very young, the elderly, the bereaved, families who feel comfortable when flying with a company that they feel knows them personally. One example that Barbara recalls is an elderly grandmother who wanted to bring her granddaughter over from Canada after she was bereaved. Barbara helped to ensure that all the arrangements would run smoothly and now the lady and her granddaughter fly Virgin whenever they can.

Donna Griffin, In-flight Development Supervisor with Virgin, whose responsibilities include supervision of in-flight services, says that she enjoys just chatting with passengers whenever she has a chance. She feels that they appreciate the human face that this reveals. Indeed, one of Richard Branson's guiding principles is that he *encourages his staff to bring their personalities to work with them.*

The staff feel that 'Richard' certainly brings his personality to work and it permeates through every department.

We mentioned earlier that all of the Virgin aircraft have individual names and this also encourages customers to view the aeroplanes as personalities too. In fact, the public have even been invited to name some of them through national newspaper competitions.

The theory behind this is that if you have the right staff and you encourage them to behave naturally, then passengers will respond. Donna says that it works very well and it encourages the staff to interact naturally with their customers.

It is very noticeable that whenever members of staff talk about the chairman, they refer to him as 'Richard' and not 'Mr Branson'. Staff, directors and chairman are on first-name terms and the result is that the staff feel that the senior people are accessible and will listen to what they have to say.

Passengers often reward staff by writing letters of praise or giving excellent feedback on flight feedback forms. All such praise is recorded on the personal file of the staff member involved. Passengers are even able to recommend particularly helpful staff for awards.

In some cases, where there has been outstanding service, letters are copied to the chairman and he will ring the staff member up personally to congratulate him or her.

This can be particularly motivating for staff. Frederick Herzberg, a famous management theorist, put forward a model of staff motivation, in which he refers to what he describes as *hygiene factors*, such as:

- The organization's policies and administration
- Styles of supervision and management
- Relationships with superiors
- Money
- Status
- Security

Hygiene factors merely prevent dissatisfaction rather than actually motivating people. On the other hand, *motivators*, such as:

- Achievement
- Recognition for skills and achievement

- The work itself
- Responsibility
- Advancement and promotion

are likely to lead to high degrees of motivation.

Clearly, Richard Branson is using at least one of Herzberg's motivators here.

Earlier in this volume, we looked at the work done by Peters and Waterman and their eight attributes of an excellent company. One of these attributes mentions 'productivity through people'. It is very important that an organization values and invests in its staff. Throughout this volume, we have been talking about focusing on the customer. Some organizations interpret this to mean that you should value only the customer and it doesn't matter about your own staff. However, in a truly excellent company, staff will be viewed as internal customers, as we mentioned in chapter 2.

As we saw in chapter 3, excellence and quality are deeply permeated into the culture of an excellent organization, and it is unlikely that a company which does not value its internal customers will be able to value its external customers.

Virgin certainly shows evidence of valuing its staff, not only by passing on compliments to them but also by the investment that is made in their training, in particular in connection with customer service.

Intensive induction training is complemented by regular training courses for all levels of staff. Recently, various departments such as cabin crew, engineers and ground services staff have undergone training at the same location so that they can meet and network during intervals in their respective courses.

GOLDEN RULE

Treat internal customers as you would external ones.

Virgin has a range of lounges for Upper Class passengers to use on departure and arrival, and there is also a clubhouse at Heathrow, which has a wide variety of facilities for Upper Class passengers to enjoy. When asked how she measures the performance of her staff in respect of customer satisfaction, Sarah Stoddart, Clubhouse Supervisor, said that one of the things she does is to look at how the passengers and the staff appear to be feeling. If they all look miserable, the chances are that there is a high degree of dissatisfaction. On the other hand, it is likely that if the staff are looking relaxed and content, this will be transmitted to the customers and vice versa.

She gives an example. An exhausted looking inbound passenger from Oman was going on to New York. He was slumped in a chair and looking dreadful. The clubhouse staff rallied round, arranged a shower and a massage, got him breakfast and arranged lunch later. Meanwhile, they found that he had been booked on a late flight in error and there was an earlier one to New York, so they booked him on that. He was transformed into a very happy man.

Sarah feels that it is important to focus on the customer and to see things from his or her point of view.

GOLDEN RULE

If you don't look after your customers, somebody else will.

In previous chapters we have looked at how important marketing is in identifying who your customers are and targeting your products at them. So far in this chapter we have seen how important the actual production or operation of the service or product is in encouraging the customer to build up a relationship with the supplier.

Let's look at other areas of the operations process where communicating with the customer is important. There are a number of ways in which communication can be carried out:

- Formal liaison meetings
- Informal meetings
- Altering arrangements
- Feedback
- General information
- Written communication

- Communicating quickly
- Individual body language
- Team body language
- Organizational body language

Let's look at each in turn.

Formal liaison meetings

Many organizations have regular meetings with their customers to discuss issues such as quality, delivery, future developments etc.

It is not unusual for management training companies, for example, to have a quarterly progress meeting to discuss these issues as well as the progress of their participants.

Home Housing, a provider of rented housing, which we will meet in more detail later, has a range of formal meetings with its tenants who are its customers. Home Housing has six geographical regions. In the three established regions (where it started its work in the 1930s) there are four representative groups meeting three times a year. This practice will extend to the emerging regions in the course of time.

Agendas include any items the tenants wish to discuss, as well as covering news of new developments being carried out by Home Housing. Each meeting is followed up with an 'action sheet', which is circulated within ten days. These Tenants' Associations elect people to the Tenants' Forum, a national body representing all of Home's tenants, which meets three times a year.

In this way, Home gets to know all of the issues that are of concern to its customers and tries to put them right.

Alan Kilburn, the Chief Executive, is very proud of these meetings, which have been held since 1976. Interestingly, up to thirty members of staff regularly attend these meetings unpaid because they want to know what the current issues are. The meetings are chaired by the Chairman or Vice-Chairman of the Board and other Board members attend. This demonstrates the value of the meetings to the landlord, the supplier, as well as to the tenant, the customer.

Alan recounts an anecdote of the importance of communication.

He coins a nice phrase – 'Our house, your home' – as a way of describing Home Housing's relationship with its tenants.

He was in an area of Sunderland after attending a meeting when a lady approached him.

'You're Mr Kilburn, aren't you?'

Having at first been very pleased to have been recognized, he was slightly disconcerted to be told of a long-running problem that was upsetting the residents of the estate. Youths were playing football late at night and crashing the ball against walls and windows and generally causing a nuisance. 'What are you going to do about it?'

'Well, I think this is a matter for the police really.'

'Yes, we've tried that. They turn up, roll up their sleeves and join in the game. Apparently it's called Community Policing.'

Alan was rather at a loss at this response, but before he could summon up a reply the lady went on, 'You remember your slogan, Our House, Your Home? Well that's all very well, but remember this. It may be my home but it's your house, now get something done about it!'

And he did!

Informal meetings

Informal meetings can be a very good way of cementing relationships with customers and can form a very valuable part of the Value Chain, which we will look at in more detail in chapter 6.

Informal meetings can be used to discuss problems and can be especially effective if they are held before things start to go wrong, rather than after they have been left to become a major problem.

They can also be useful from the point of view that we mentioned earlier, in that they allow you to get to know your customers and let them build up a trust in you. They give you a chance to get to know their names – and allow customers to get to know yours.

Alan Kilburn of Home Housing points out that it is not only important for you to know your customers' names, but also very powerful if they know yours. He is very keen that the tenants have a clear idea of who their local Home Housing contact is, by name and preferably by having met them.

Altering arrangements

In every organization at some time, arrangements that you have made with your customer will need to be changed. This may be for any number of reasons, but the important thing is to tell the client what is happening, and preferably why, and try to agree a new arrangement. If you have a lot of customers, like transport organizations, for example, you may not be able to discuss it with them, but at the very least you can inform them so that they can make alternative arrangements where necessary.

This may seem very obvious but it is something which does not always happen, even where personal customers are involved and they could be contacted. For example, have you ever made arrangements to take time off work in order to be in the house either to accept a delivery or to have a home repair carried out? Almost everyone has a story of this happening and then no one turning up. Or a taxi fails to turn up at the appointed time. You ring the company only to be told that they are running late. Well, they have your telephone number and they have permanent contact with their driver, so why can't they ring and tell you before you have to ring them?

HOWLER

A motorist is driving down the motorway after a three-hour drive and he has now arrived in his own county. He can take any of the next three exits to get home, but the most direct exit is the second one. He should be home in twenty minutes. He drives past the first exit, goes round a sharp bend and immediately comes to a sign that says 'Road Works Ahead 3 Miles'. Two hundred yards in front of him is the back of the queue. One and a half hours later he arrives home.

Had he been given advance warning, he would have taken the first exit and arrived home about an hour earlier than he did.

HOWLER

A passenger on a train somewhere in the world. He has been on the train for five hours and the train has stopped at the last station before his stop. It is thirty minutes to his destination. His wife is going to pick him up at the station and will be leaving in about ten minutes. He wonders whether he should phone her on the mobile and tell her that the train looks as if it will be on time. He decides not to bother as there is no change to the arrangements.

Half-way to the final stop the train grinds to a halt. After some ten minutes the conductor speaks through the train and tells everyone that there will be a delay of thirty minutes because all of the signals have failed due to an electrical storm *last night* – that is, some twenty-four hours ago!

Had the passenger known a few minutes earlier he could have told his wife to set off later. And the conductor and his colleagues had known since last night!

When he did finally arrive home he telephoned the relatives he had been visiting to tell them he was safe.

'I expect you were delayed,' said his aunt. 'The travel news on the radio said there was a thirty minute delay on that line'.

So the information was known to everyone except the passengers on the train!

Feedback

Feedback from customers is very important, whether you ask them formally through questionnaires or whether it arrives through casual conversation, customer queries or complaints. We saw earlier how effectively Virgin uses its Top Ten issues. It is vital that when you have the feedback you *act* on it! We will look at service recovery and dealing with complaints in the next chapter. For the time being, however, we should remember that feedback is a form of market research. It tells you how your customer views your product. It may even tell you what innovations you might profitably make! Market research is expensive; feedback may even be offered *free*!

It is also extremely important that you pass on compliments to the appropriate staff, as this can be very motivating – as we saw earlier in the Virgin Atlantic example.

One of the most neglected areas in customer relations is that of feedback between internal customers. This is because it is often seen as moaning between departments rather than proper feedback. Remember, it is important what your internal customers think of you too!

Some of the more progressive organizations now carry out a periodic staff feedback exercise on how they, the staff, perceive the organization, and this information can prove to be very instructive.

General information

In some customer relationships things will be happening most effectively when there is little need for further communication between customer and supplier. In such cases it is likely that the customer will have bought the product and there will be excellent instructions on how to use it or on how to assemble it.

We have all found examples when things have not worked so smoothly. For example, computer hardware and software often arrives without sufficiently clear instructions to indicate set-up procedures.

HOWLER

A client bought a computer from a well-known firm. It arrived with no manuals and no instructions indicating what went where. Half of the software was loaded and half was not. Not surprisingly, the company has since gone out of business.

It is not enough just to have instructions clearly included inside the packaging. It is no good the customer buying something and ripping off the packaging only to find that he does not have either the tools or the skills to assemble it.

HOWLER

A lady purchased a medicine boot for her horse, who was suffering from an abscess under its foot. The boot was in a shrink-wrapped package with the instructions on the inside, where she couldn't read them. She asked the assistant if there was anything else she would need to go with the boot and was told that there wasn't.

On arriving home and opening the package, it became clear from the instructions that three foam wedges were required to pack the boot before putting it onto the horse's foot. The American manufacturers sold these separately. On phoning the shop, the lady was told that these wedges were not available in England!

In many cases there are supplementary items that can be bought to go with a main purchase, or you can buy replacements for parts of it that wear out. Again, finding the correct part can be a nightmare.

HOWLER

A man goes into a supermarket to buy some razor blades for his razor. He knows the brand name and thinks it will be a simple matter to identify what he wants. He is confronted with a range of blades made by several different manufacturers. He purchases a pack of razors that look as though they resemble his previous blades. He returns home and opens the pack. They don't fit his razor. He takes them back to the supermarket but the manager refuses to change them because he has opened the packaging.

In a world in which market segmentation is vital, it is often necessary to have a range of products to suit different needs. However, it should be quite clear to your customers which product they should be looking for. Remember, this is not the customer's problem in the long run; it is *your* problem.

THINK POINT

Can you be sure that your products do not fall into this trap? If they do, what can you do about it?

GOLDEN RULE

Dissatisfied customers have far more friends than satisfied ones.

Written communication

There are times when you need to put something in writing to formalize a situation. This may include formal arrangements, contracts, dealing with complaints, feedback forms etc. The main point here is that it should be very clear and not open to other interpretations.

Written communication also allows a record to be kept of what has happened. In many cases, today, although the letter is physically sent, copies are retained in computer files.

Newspapers and newsletters can be very good ways of keeping your customers informed about what is happening in your company. Home Housing sends out a regular newspaper, called *Home Scene*, to all of its 25 000 tenants, in which it highlights new developments and takes the opportunity to foster a family atmosphere by featuring events and people and special occasions. Home also has an internal staff newspaper called *At Home*.

Communicating quickly
Often you will need to communicate quickly with your customers. In today's high tech world you have a number of choices:

- Telephone
- Fax
- Electronic mail
- Video conferencing

Let's look at each in turn.

Telephone

A tried, and in many cases not to be trusted, method of communicating – you have no body language to confirm what your ears are hearing; you have no written confirmation of what has been agreed; the tone of the conversation can be difficult to gauge; humour can easily be misunderstood.

Having said that, the telephone, when used wisely, can be a very quick and effective manner of communicating with your customer.

Fax

As mentioned in chapter 2, the fax machine is now widespread and can be a very effective means of transmitting documents or other written information quickly.

Electronic mail

As the use of electronic mail becomes ever more common, it can be a very useful means of communication. When used to pass a message to several people at the same time it becomes more versatile than the fax.

Care does need to be taken, however. The message, when sent, is not always copied to the sender's machine, so a record of what was sent may not be available. Messages may be sent according to a prearranged mailing list and you may not always want everyone on that list to receive the message. You may realize this too late.

Email can also stifle personal interaction, with the result that people stop talking to each other and send brief, impersonal notes instead. In recognition of this, protocols are being introduced to make email more interactive by the use of special symbols, known as smileys.

If used with care, however, it can be very powerful. Currently it is probably used more between internal customers. However, this is changing, with more and more organizations seeing the value of being able to communicate with customers or suppliers in this way.

Video conferencing

With video conferencing you can have a meeting without everyone having to travel. This can be particularly effective if the parties who need to communicate are located a long way from each other. The major difficulty at the moment is that relatively few organizations have the capability to use the system.

Video conferencing does allow body language to come back into the communication, although some people do not relax and their body language may be confused.

Individual body language

If you doubt in any way the power of body language, a good exercise is to watch a play or a sitcom on television with the sound turned down. If the actors are good, it is surprising how much you can follow even though you cannot hear any words.

On the other hand, try listening to the sound only and see how much you miss.

One of the main problems with body language is that it can mean different things in different cultures. What might be explanatory in one culture may be downright insulting in another. Many organizations that deal with a variety of cultures offer specific training in this area.

The important thing here is to recognize this fact and think consciously of the impression you are making.

A salesperson may well find that he or she has made or lost a sale before even saying a word!

Team body language

It is also possible for teams to have a body language all of their own. This can often be observed in close-knit task groups, where there may be 'in' jargon or 'in' jokes that outsiders cannot appreciate. They may well only maintain eye contact or address their conversation to members of the inner sanctum, and may in extreme cases practically turn their backs on outsiders.

THINK POINT

If you are part of a team, the next time that you and the rest of the team are meeting other groups or socializing, try to observe your own team's (and the other team's) body language. You may find it interesting.

Organizational body language

Linked closely with individual and team body language is what the authors like to call organizational body language, which relates to the whole atmosphere that an organization creates. In short, there are those organizations that welcome customers and with whom it is a pleasure to do business, and those with whom it is an endurance test.

When you visit a welcoming organization, there is likely to be a pleasant place to sit. You may be offered coffee by a friendly member of staff and invited to sit and wait in a comfortable chair. Or there may be magazines to read while you are waiting. Or you may even be shown in immediately for your appointment!

On the other hand, you may encounter any of the following:

- You drive to the company and there is no car parking space.
- You arrive at the door and it is locked.
- You enter and there is nobody there.
- There is somebody there, but with their back to you.
- There is somebody there but he or she walks off as you approach.
- There are two people there but they are interested in each other, not you.
- There is a large queue and only one person is serving while lots of others are walking about doing other things.
- There is loud music blaring, which you find unbearable.
- There is someone at reception but nowhere to sit and wait.
- Although you have made an appointment, the receptionist has never heard of you.
- You telephone and no one answers.
- You leave a message on an answering machine and no one calls you back.
- No one answers your letters.

And then perhaps the worst of all:

- You arrive in reception and no one has ever heard of the person you have arranged to see!

Another example of organizational body language would be a shop that doesn't display any prices on the expensive looking products in its windows!

Outstanding organizations will usually pay close attention to this organizational body language. The important point is to approach your own organization as if you were an external customer. Does it welcome people or not? If it does, people are likely to come back again, if not . . .

A good example of a company that pays close attention to this aspect is the Little Chef group of restaurants, which has written objectives for its staff to meet. They are also posted at the entrance for customers to see. They spell out quite clearly the standards that staff are expected to meet in respect of such things as:

- greeting customers
- how long before they are given the menu and their first drink
- asking customers if they enjoyed their meal etc.

With any of the types of body language the halo/horns effect will apply. If it is open and welcoming, people will assume that this reflects the rest of the organization (halo). If it is the opposite (horns), then they will assume the worst.

There is a sound version of the halo/horns effect. If you overhear someone talking about an organization, this is likely to influence you. If you hear them saying good things it is likely to tempt you to try the product, while bad things are likely to put you off.

Next time you are talking over coffee with a colleague in a public place, remember that your conversation may be overheard by that potential customer whom the marketing director has spent the past six months persuading to buy your product. A chance remark about how poor your despatch department is could undo all those months of hard work!

Another aspect of organizational body language is communicating very negatively. You may have seen notices on market stalls such as 'Don't pick out the fruit'.

Other things you might see are:

- Don't lean on the counter
- No credit

- No cheques
- No refunds
- Broken counts as sold
- Do not touch
- No push chairs
- No food
- No children
- No dogs
- No cameras
- Keep off
- No change for car park
- No bags beyond this point

If your organization has to make these exhortations – and there may be good reasons why it might need to – it is best to phrase them in a positive manner, or at least phrase them as requests, such as:

- For security reasons please leave your bags with the attendant

Customers who meet a barrage of prohibition notices are likely to interpret this as 'Go away, you're too much trouble' and they are likely to take the hint!

GOLDEN RULE

If you don't look after your customers, somebody else will.

Remember, negative or no communication *is* communication!

A further significant aspect of organizational body language is smell.

At first glance, this may appear to be an odd thing to mention but it can be a very powerful method of communication. For example, there is a shop in Cirencester that sells coffee beans and accessories, as well as having a coffee bar. The aroma of coffee as you walk by makes it almost impossible to resist entering.

The Belvedere pork shop, a small delicatessen in Whitley Bay, makes the most delicious pork pies, and the aroma when they first arrive hot in the shop is irresistible. Other examples include bakers' shops in any high street, where the smell of bread baking draws in the clientele.

We think most people know of the ruse when trying to sell your house. Put on a brew of fresh coffee in the percolator, which gives the house a wonderful aura and may well sway any prospective purchasers.

On the other hand, there have been some examples of the opposite.

HOWLER

There is an excellent pub/restaurant that attracts a wide range of customers for its varied menu and delicious cooking. Unfortunately, the restaurant still has a septic tank, which can smell rather offensive outside, which means that when entering and leaving you have to hold your breath, while the beer garden rarely gets used!

HOWLER

There is at least one recently built hotel that offers fantastic facilities, including an indoor swimming pool and health spa. Unfortunately, it is built next to a sewage works!

Communicating with your customers means very much more than just telling them what you think is important. It is usually described as a two-way process, which involves listening as well as informing, as can be seen in figure 12.

This is really too simplistic a description because it remains a

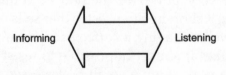

Informing   Listening

Figure 12 Two-way communication

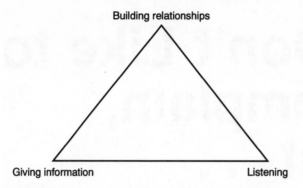

Figure 13 The three dimensions of communication

rather two-dimensional one. In this chapter we have suggested that there is much more to it than this. Communication, we believe, should be at least a three-dimensional process, in which building a relationship with your customer provides the third dimension and is likely to be the most effective at ensuring that communication continues in the future. Please see the diagram in figure 13.

In fact, we would argue that there is a fourth dimension, in which not only do you build a relationship, but you begin to work together with your customers to help them to meet their own vital success factors as part of a value chain. We will look at this fourth dimension in chapter 6.

SUMMARY

In this chapter we have looked at the role of communication and have introduced concepts of building relationships and individual/team/organizational body language and their importance to effective customer service.

5

I Don't Like to Complain, but . . .

COMPLAINTS, FEEDBACK AND RECOVERY

In every organization there are bound to be times when things don't turn out as expected. In fact, things may well go completely wrong. It is rarely the *fact* that something goes wrong that causes customers to be lost, but rather the way in which the organization responds to it.

So, in this chapter we are going to look at how organizations might respond. This is usually referred to as *service recovery*. In this volume we will call it 'customer recovery', because that really is the crucial issue.

Let's first ask a very basic question: why bother with customer recovery at all?

Let's consider a young person of about eighteen years of age. She has some 42 years of working life ahead, in which, with luck, she will be earning money to enable her to live and purchase the usual range of items that people buy. In that 42 years she might buy anything up to:

- fifteen cars (£150 000)
- mortgage repayments (£400 000 or rent of £90 000)
- two thousand meals out (£10 000)
- fifty holidays (a couple might make this 100) (£25 000–50 000)
- thirty suits (£6000)
- two thousand weekly shopping baskets (£100 000)
- four hundred plants or shrubs for the garden (£2000)
- four hundred compact discs (£4800)

- two thousand bottles of wine (£8000)

Hopefully, when she retires she will enjoy a long and happy time with a fully funded pension, and it is likely that her reduced spending power will be matched by reduced expenses that still leave her with some discretionary purchasing power to spend on whatever she enjoys.

As you can see, these are very large stakes that organizations are playing for. A very satisfied customer might tell one or two people how pleased he or she is, but research has shown that a dissatisfied one is likely to tell on average ten other people about the bad experience. So let's look at the risks and opportunities.

A large supermarket chain risks losing some £100 000 worth of revenue if it loses our eighteen-year-old, but it will earn that much if it keeps her loyal.

A travel agency puts at risk some £25 000–50 000 worth of revenue, while a car dealer risks some £150 000. Even for small businesses, the stakes can be high when such a long-term view is taken. A corner shop where our eighteen-year-old may spend some £3 per week stands to risk some £6300. Customer recovery becomes a very important issue if this 'lifetime value of a customer' approach is taken. The additional costs that might (but not always) be incurred by customer recovery need to be viewed against the 'lifetime cost' of losing him or her.

Of course, there may be many reasons why an organization might lose customers that are nothing to do with poor service, such as moving away from the area or changing tastes or jobs. However, in these instances you have no opportunity to retain their custom unless, perhaps, you work for a national chain. The difference with poor service is that you do have the opportunity to do something about it. It is in your own hands!

So what is customer recovery? One definition might be:

Turning disaster into a triumph.

Most customers, especially if you have worked on building up a relationship as mentioned in chapter 4, will give you another chance provided you take the appropriate action. Indeed, you may well be able to enhance your relationship rather than see it diminish, depending upon how you deal with the situation, in which case you will have achieved the triumph mentioned in our definition above. Having said that, the wrong action or no action may well leave you gazing only on the disaster!

GOOD EXAMPLE

Let's look at a good example of turning disaster into triumph.

A man and his wife met a couple they knew in the local pub. It turned out that they had both been visiting New Zealand during the summer at roughly the same time without realizing it. They asked them which airline they had used. 'Singapore Airlines'.
'What were they like?'
'Fantastic!'
'In what way?'
'Well, we set off from Heathrow and within an hour we had to land at Amsterdam. Then we had to fly back to Heathrow because the fault couldn't be rectified in Amsterdam. It was about twelve hours . . .'
'Hold on, Bill, are you serious? They give you all this hassle and you say they're fantastic?'
'Well, yes, they were. At every stage they told us exactly what was happening and what was being done to try to rectify the problem. They gave us plenty of food and plenty to drink and generally looked after us so well that I don't believe they could have done anything more for us. After all, anyone can have a problem, but the real difference is how they deal with it. You can be sure that I'll be flying with Singapore Airlines whenever I get the opportunity.'
'Well, we flew with another airline and they got us there on time and quite safely but I wouldn't say that we would always use that airline. Singapore have certainly made quite an impression on you!'

As you can see, the organization came out of the situation better than one of its competitors, which provided a perfectly adequate service and didn't have any problems at all!

One thing that needs to be remembered is that the way you deal with any situation is unlikely to depend wholly on the rights and wrongs of the situation as you – that is, the representative of the organization – see it. You need to look at any situation from your customer's point of view. Let's look at some situations where you might be called upon to carry out a customer recovery.

1   You know what has gone wrong and it is your organization's fault.
2   You know what has gone wrong and you don't think it is your organization's fault.
3   It's not your fault and you don't know whose fault it is, or it was beyond your control.
4   You do know whose fault it is.
5   You can't believe the customer expected that particular service.
6   You don't know that anything has gone wrong. The customer walks away and never uses you again.

Now we are going to look, under each of these categories, at some actual examples of customer recovery carried out by real organizations. In each case, the situation will be explained. You will then be invited to suggest what the organization should do, if anything. We will then tell you what the organization actually did. We will leave it to you to decide whether the organization was successful or not.

1   You know what has gone wrong and it is your organization's fault

Let's look at an example:

A client peruses the menu in a hotel restaurant. He decides to order a steak. There are a number of dishes to choose from, such as rump, sirloin or fillet steak, and many sauces on offer too, but his favourite is sirloin cooked medium rare so that is what he orders.

The meal arrives and the waitress puts down the plate in front of the guest.

'Excuse me, this looks like a fillet steak and I ordered a sirloin.'

'Well, I wouldn't know, I never eat them, but I'll check with the chef.'

She returns about three minutes later. 'The chef says that it's definitely a sirloin.'

The guest looks round. He is the only person in the dining room this late in the evening so it cannot be a case of getting the wrong table number.

'Well, OK, but it certainly looks like a fillet to me!'

He finishes the meal and the waitress returns to clear away the plate and offer a sweet. 'Was everything all right?'

'OK. I suppose, except that the steak was definitely a fillet. I do know the difference in taste and texture and looks! I ordered a sirloin because I prefer it and would much rather have had a sirloin, as I ordered.'

Five minutes later the chef comes out to the table and admits that it was a fillet and not a sirloin steak.

THINK POINT

What would you do now as the restaurant manager or person in charge to recover the situation?

You might have suggested any number of options here, including:

- Not charging for the meal
- Offering the guest a free breakfast next morning
- Apologizing profusely
- Reducing the price of the meal

What actually happened was as follows.

The chef apologised and explained that the price of the fillet steak was some £2 higher than that of the sirloin. As the client had ordered the sirloin he would only be charged for the sirloin. He was, in fact, said the chef, getting a good deal because he had eaten a superior piece of meat.

'But I wanted a sirloin!' retorted the exasperated guest, who has never stayed or eaten at the hotel since.

Triumph or disaster? Has the organization looked at it from the customer's point of view?

Let's take another example.

A lady booked a room at a hotel a few days in advance. When

she made the reservation she checked that the room was quiet and suitable for a business lady staying on her own. She was assured that it was. When she arrived, she found that her room was in an annexe on the opposite side of a busy road, above a noisy discotheque.

In the annexe, there was no reception and no restaurant facilities. This meant that she had to cross the road late in the evening when it was dark in a strange city. The annexe entrance was shared with the discotheque.

Feeling rather dubious about all this but having being told that there were no other rooms available, she felt she had no option but to accept it.

She ran a bath but found that she could not open the plastic packaging of the soap. She dried off and decided to ring reception. There was no phone!

Having finished her bath without the soap, she dressed for dinner and crossed the busy road to the restaurant. She called in at reception to tell them about the soap packaging.

'Yes, all of our customers have that problem. We bring our own soap in from home for our own use. We haven't any phones in the annexe rooms but all of those in the main building have them.'

The manager promised to call out his handyman, who was quite used to opening the packaging with his screwdriver.

After dinner, she collected the soap from the handyman and crossed the busy road in the dark to return to her quiet room, which was by this time reverberating to the sounds of the discotheque below.

She decide to have another bath, this time armed with the soap, and then try to get some sleep.

She entered the bathroom, closed the door and had her bath.

After drying off, she discovered that there was no handle on the inside of the bathroom door!

So, let's take stock of her situation.

She has only a towel, because her clothes are in the other room. She is locked in the bathroom with no telephone communication with reception, which is across the road. No one can hear her shouting because of the noise from the disco.

She sat on the floor in a wet towel for some three hours. Earlier she had tried to squeeze her fingers under the door to try to ease it towards her but the condensation in the bathroom meant that the bottom of the door was too wet and her fingers just slid off.

After about three hours she was able to get more of a grip on the bottom of the door, which had now dried out, and at last she pulled it open.

Even now she could not vent her anger on anyone as there was no phone in the room, and she desperately needed to get some sleep as she had an important meeting in the morning!

THINK POINT

If you were the manager, how would you handle her complaint in the morning?

The options here are too numerous to list!

Thankfully, it is not very often that such a catalogue of disasters occurs at the same time. As you can imagine, the manager was horrified to hear of the lady's problems.

What actually happened was that he didn't charge the lady for the room or for her meal in the restaurant, although he did charge her for the half bottle of wine she drank with it. He offered a free room for one night if she cared to return, and assured her that she would be accommodated in the main building.

If she returns to that city she intends to give them another chance and take him up on his offer.

> **Triumph or disaster? Has the organization looked at it from the customer's point of view?**

Perhaps before we move on we should consider an eleventh golden rule: 'Always check that there is a handle on the inside of the bathroom door before you close it!'

---

2 You know what has gone wrong and you don't think it is your organization's fault

A man went into a supermarket and complained about some prawns that he had bought last weekend.

'Have you brought them back?'

'No, they were off when I bought them and today is the first opportunity to come into the store since then. I couldn't have kept off prawns all this time.'

'Did you keep the receipt?'

'No, I don't keep grocery receipts, do you?'

The lady at the counter went to fetch the manager. She could not be sure whether the complaint was genuine or not. After all, anyone could say they had bought something that was off last week, and he didn't have a receipt to confirm that he had even bought anything at all.

THINK POINT

If you were the manager what would you have done? The value of the prawns was £2.50.

This is a tricky one on the face of it.
You might have suggested

- refunding the money
- or giving him some more prawns
- or doing nothing as he could not prove anything

The problem becomes easier when you refer back to the lifetime value of the customer. There could be up to £100 000 at risk here!

What the manager actually did was to say that he would consider the matter and write to the man, and asked him for his address. He then sent the customer a refund of £2.20, with no explanation as to why he was not refunding the whole amount.

The customer was not impressed and although he still uses the store, because it is convenient, he no longer uses it for his main weekly shop. This 30p saving does not seem good value for the store manager!

Triumph or disaster? Has the organization looked at it from the customer's point of view?

Let's take another example.

A woman goes into a high street shop and looks for a particular type of photograph album. It is the type where you can buy the outer cover and the inner leaves separately so that you can make the album any size you like. The store had the leaves in stock but not the outer covers. She enquired at the counter and was told that not only were they out of stock but they were being discontinued.

She thought about this for a moment and then reasoned that, although they were going to be discontinued there would probably be a few around in the shops for a while, so she would go to another branch and buy an outer cover there. So she bought some £35 worth of inner leaves.

During the next few weeks she visited four different branches and could not find a cover. A little worried, she wrote to the head office explaining that she had thought that she would be able to find some but so far her search had been fruitless. She suggested that there must still be one or two left somewhere in the country. If the head office could locate one and have it sent to her she would gladly pay a little extra for their trouble. She was at pains to point out that it was her own fault for buying the leaves and that she had been quite clearly told that they would be discontinued but she had decided to take a chance.

THINK POINT

If you had been the Head Office Manager responsible, how would you have handled this?

There are a number of options here:

- You could write back without asking any branches, in order to avoid extra work, and say that you are very sorry but there are none left.
- You could ask the branches and send her one if one could be found or advise her as before that there are none left.
- If you send her one, you could charge her the normal price, make an extra charge for the extra work you've done, or give it to her free because they are no longer on sale anyway.

Whatever you decide, you need to remember that you did have

the items on sale, even though your staff did issue a warning. For you to be completely in the right you should probably have withdrawn them from sale.

What actually happened was that a couple of weeks later the woman received a very polite note saying that they had looked everywhere but there were none to be found. A cheque refunding her £35 was enclosed with the letter, which also expressed the hope that she could find some use for the inner leaves, which she was welcome to keep.

Triumph or disaster? Has the organization looked at it from the customer's point of view?

3   It's not your fault and you don't know whose fault it is, or it was beyond your control

It is midnight on an aeroplane that is an hour and a half into a six-hour journey. The cabin crew are serving a light meal. Just as the last meal is served the 'seat belt' signs go on and the captain's voice can be heard warning of severe turbulence and telling the cabin crew to stop serving, go to their seats and fasten their belts too!

One of the passengers clings onto the meal he has just been served and can be heard remarking to his wife, 'Do you think I should try to eat this or should I just cut out the middle man and empty it straight into the sick bag?'

After about half an hour normal service is resumed, although most passengers have eaten very little.

THINK POINT

Should the cabin crew do anything?

You might think that turbulence can be expected on aeroplanes and neither the cabin crew nor the airline can do much about it.

What actually happened was that the cabin crew came round and offered a glass of champagne to everyone to cheer them up. Although the situation wasn't their fault, they took ownership of the tense atmosphere on the plane and tried, successfully, to do something about it.

Triumph or disaster? Has the organization looked at it from the customer's point of view?

Let's take another example.

A lady who was a very good cook won a prize in a cookery competition with a national newspaper. The prize was four de luxe hampers of wine and food, which would be sent out at quarterly intervals during the year.

The first three arrived and the lady was delighted with them. The last was due a few weeks before Christmas. She waited and waited but it didn't arrive.

She telephoned the newspaper and was told that it wasn't the newspaper's fault because the hampers were provided by a subcontractor who had gone out of business. The lady reminded the representative of the newspaper that this was their problem and they should honour their commitment and use another supplier. After some heated discussion the representative eventually agreed that the final one would be sent.

It duly arrived but, to her horror, the lady found that a bottle of port had broken inside the hamper. She telephoned the newspaper again to tell them what had happened. She explained that although it was all a bit of a mess, most of the hamper was recoverable because the items were in individual tins or bottles and were therefore undamaged.

THINK POINT

What would you do if you were the newspaper representative? The hampers were a prize and the lady did not therefore pay anything for them. Your subcontractor has already caused you some inconvenience and now your delivery agents have caused some damage to the final hamper.

Options might include:

- Asking the delivery people to deliver a new hamper and collect the damaged one.
- Sending a bottle of port as a replacement and suggesting that the lady use the undamaged items.
- Doing nothing and hope she gets fed up with it all.

What actually happened was that the representative sent her a replacement hamper and told her that she was welcome to keep any of the items she could salvage from the first. The lady had an exceptional Christmas that year!

However, she was so annoyed by the company's initial response that this was still not enough to make her feel comfortable with them, so she no longer takes that newspaper.

Triumph or disaster? Has the organization looked at it from the customer's point of view?

4 You do know whose fault it is

There is a Howler earlier in the book in which a guest arrives in the middle of the night at a hotel in Darwin only to find that it is overbooked and he has to move to another hotel for the night. He has another five nights at the hotel, which can accommodate him on these nights.

THINK POINT

What, if anything should the hotel manager/tour operator do?

There are any number of options here. You might have suggested:

- upgrading the room
- upgrading and offering some free meals or free excursions
- refunding one night's money

What actually happened is that the guest was upgraded to a suite. The guest felt that this was not enough and contacted the tour operator. She promised to investigate. She responded in due course that as it was the hotel's fault, it was up to them to deal with it and not her. As they were now satisfied, she was satisfied.

'So everyone is satisfied except me,' said the customer, who has never used either the hotel or the tour operator again.

> **Triumph or disaster? Has the organization looked at it from the customer's point of view?**

5   You can't believe the customer expected that particular service

Passengers are sitting on an aeroplane waiting to take off for Paris. The last passengers to arrive appear rather breathless and take their seats. They have just connected from a delayed local service from Newcastle.

On this particular service no refreshments are being offered. The flight only lasts some 50 minutes.

When they are airborne, one of the late arrivals says to one of the cabin crew, 'Excuse me, but we have been travelling for quite a long time and we haven't been offered a drink for several hours. Do you think we could have a cup of tea?'

THINK POINT

A dilemma for the cabin crew member? What would you have done?

This is not straightforward: it would be very easy to offer this particular lady a cup of tea; however, many other passengers may well be in a similar situation, and if they all made a request the cabin crew would not be able to satisfy them.

One way out of it might have been to say, 'Yes, you do look a little unwell. I'll tell you what, I'll bring you a cup of tea.'

What actually happened was that the staff member said, 'I'm sorry, madam, but if I get one for you, then everyone else will want one.'

This example is from a few years ago and now, because of

fierce competition, most airlines serve refreshments even on short flights.

Triumph or disaster? Has the organization looked at it from the customer's point of view?

6 *You don't know that anything has gone wrong. The customer walks away and never uses you again*

A man is driving to an important appointment when his car breaks down. He is about fifty metres from a petrol station, which also sells new and used cars, but does not carry out repairs. He goes into the office of the petrol station and asks to use the telephone, first to ring his appointment and then to ring the nearest repair garage.

THINK POINT

Again, this is a tricky one. The man is not even your customer but he could be a potential one. Would you let him use the telephone? Or is there any other way you could help?

Common courtesy would suggest that you offer to help by letting him use the phone. If you had a contact in the repair trade you might well have telephoned him on the man's behalf.

What actually happened was that he was told, 'I'm sorry, I'm waiting for an important call and anyway, we only allow customers to use our facilities'.

The man eventually sorted things out without their help.

The repair to his car turned out to be rather expensive so he decided to buy a new one. Guess where he didn't look for one! *And in the lifetime stakes he still has another five cars to go!*

Triumph or disaster? Has the organization looked at it from the potential customer's point of view?

Some of these examples are particularly interesting in that the organization has gone some way towards customer recovery but the customer has not been retained. It is a matter of fine judgement, and the company will not always get it right. Clearly, this is important because if you invest in some degree of customer recovery and still lose the customer you are getting the worst of all worlds.

So let's now take a look at how you can increase your chances of making an effective customer recovery:

1 In some cases a simple apology is enough
2 You could signal what you intend to do in advance
3 You might have a specialist customer service department
4 You could devolve responsibility for decision making closer to the customer
5 You could adopt a 'Winning for customers' culture by getting staff to take ownership of the customer's problem

Let's look at each in turn.

1 A simple apology

You do not always need to spend money on customer recovery. Often, a simple apology will do. Or you may take extra care of the customer next time they use your service. Airlines often make a record in a database of customers who need to be 'pampered' next time.

Donna Griffin of Virgin was asked how she dealt with 'difficult' customers.

> 'Well, I don't really like the word "difficult", because if people are "difficult" it is usually for a reason. You need to find out what that is and try to put it right. If we are advised that a passenger has had problems I never tell my staff that he or she is "difficult", because they might be afraid of upsetting them further. So when I'm flying there are no "difficult" customers, just VIPs!'

'The important thing is to talk calmly and gently to passengers and they usually respond,' adds her colleague, Sarah Stoddart.

It is possible that on some occasions you may even have to say no, in which case you need to say it nicely and explain why it is necessary.

GOLDEN RULE

The customer is not always right, but how you tell them that they're wrong can make all the difference and ultimately they do pay your wages.

2   Signalling what you intend to do in advance

In some industries there is a laid down procedure to deal with things when they go wrong. We might call it 'getting your customer recovery in first'.

Marks & Spencer allows refunds on anything purchased at one of its stores, whether it is faulty or not. Rover also says that you can return a new car to it for whatever reason, again even if it is not faulty.

Holiday insurance policies often set out exactly how much compensation will be paid for delays etc.

Several supermarket chains have introduced a 'no questions asked' refund policy.

This can be viewed as customer recovery in advance because it reassures people that even if things go wrong they will be put right.

THINK POINT

Does your organization have a laid down policy on customer recovery or complaints?

3   The customer service department

Barbara Garwood heads a specialist customer service team at Virgin headquarters. There is a wealth of experience in the team and most people have been in several parts of the organization, including the 'sharp end':

'This is important because you need to see things from the customer's perspective, to find out where they are coming from.'

The department deals with all areas of customer problems and complaints, and tries to take a proactive approach: 'If you know something is going wrong, you should try to put it right immediately. It is far better to overcome the problem than to think about compensating people later.'

If things do go wrong and cannot be put right at the time, Barbara has set down very clear response times for dealing with the subsequent complaint.

Upper Class customer complaints have to be dealt with to finality within 48 hours.

Premium Economy complaints are acknowledged immediately and should be cleared within 21 days.

Economy passengers, once again, are acknowledged and should have their complaints answered within 28 days.

The department takes a very keen interest in training and motivation. Quarterly customer service awards are given to staff for outstanding efforts. Specific customer service training is given, including cultural training where appropriate.

The department also monitors and administers the Virgin Top Ten issues, which the company finds so useful.

4 *Devolve responsibility*

The closer to the customer you take any decision, the quicker the problem is likely to be put right. Many organizations delegate authority to their front-line staff to give small presents to or make special arrangements for customers who have encountered problems.

The key here is in the training. Giving people authority without also giving them the means to use it wisely is likely to be counter-productive. It may also prove expensive!

5 A 'winning for customers' culture

This phrase was adopted by British Airways for its company-wide training programme, attended by almost the entire workforce and some of their service partners.

The main thrust was to encourage people to take responsibility for their customer.

In relation to customer recovery, this means taking a proactive role. This means that you don't just give the customer a form and tell him or her to fill it in. If a form has to be filled in, the member of staff should complete it with the customer's help.

Here are some examples of traditional behaviour contrasted with the 'taking responsibility' approach:

'You need to take a taxi from over there.'
'I'll get you a taxi.'
'You need to fill out this form and send it off to us.'
'Let's fill in this form together.'
'I think you need to talk to a supervisor.'
'I'll go and get my supervisor.'
'You can help yourself to a coffee over there.'
'I'll bring you a coffee.'

HOWLER

A lady is waiting in the casualty department of a major English hospital on a Sunday afternoon. She suspects that she has cracked a rib, so she felt that she had better have it checked out.

She sits on an uncomfortable seat for some four hours, by which time her ribs are aching like toothache. The nurse still cannot tell her when she is likely to be able to see a doctor. She and her husband decide that waiting in such discomfort is causing her more problems than not being seen so they decide to leave and go to the local health centre the following morning when it opens again.

Before they leave, the husband, who is rather cross, approaches the nurse and tells her that they are going home and asks for a complaints form.

'I'm sorry but we've run out.'

GOLDEN RULE

If you don't look after your customers, somebody else will.

As you can see from this example, taking responsibility for your customer doesn't only apply in profit making organizations. The following good example of taking ownership comes from a non-profit making organization.

GOOD EXAMPLE

Colin Garbutt of Home Housing recalled a contractor to a repair of a damp-proof course that had not been satisfactory. The tenant had encountered persistent dampness in his home, which resulted in damage to his wall coverings, furniture and carpets. The contractor responsible had tried to rectify the problem but had failed to effect improvements within a reasonable time.

Colin stepped in, and not only ensured that the repair was carried out but also negotiated, on the tenant's behalf, a compensatory sum from the contractor and a sum from the insurance company, and arranged for the house to be redecorated at the contractor's expense in the wall covering of the tenant's choice.

Whatever the situation that exists in your organization, you can be sure that customer recovery is a vital issue. The trick is in knowing how far to go in order to retain the customer while at the same time preserving the company's return on the deal. After all, you cannot give compensation to everyone.

Give too much and you lose profit; too little and you lose the customer. In the end, you need to take into account:

- the power of the customer
- the lifetime value of the customer to the organization
- the power and value of the customer's friends
- the culture of your organization
- the view of the staff member closest to the problem

Let's look at each in more detail.

The power of the customer

As we saw in chapter 2, there are some situations in which the customer has a great deal of power. This may be because the organization may have only one customer, so losing that customer would be fatal to the business. Or it may be that the customer is in a position to cause maximum public embarrassment so that the company's public image might suffer.

The lifetime value of the customer to the organization

The lifetime value will be related to the value of the product and the frequency with which it is purchased, and the length of time over which the purchase takes place. Thus, you may feel that a young customer with a frequent saver card for a particular supermarket may need more attention than an older casual purchaser. You need to remember here, however, that the customer will also have put a value on him or herself and if he or she feels that this valuation and yours are out of line, you will have a valuation gap and you are likely to lose that customer. Please see the diagram in figure 14.

One of the dangers here is that you may be dealing with a potential customer whom you have not noticed buying very much, so you assign them a relatively low value. The potential customer will assign his or her potential value and thus exacerbate the gap. So there are dangers in relying on your own perspective of the situation.

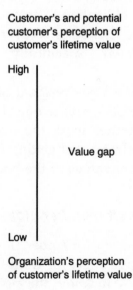

Customer's and potential
customer's perception of
customer's lifetime value

High

Value gap

Low

Organization's perception
of customer's lifetime value

Figure 14 The value gap

The power and value of the customer's friends

Another real danger of using only the perceived lifetime value is that customers have friends and acquaintances. If you fail to satisfy a customer whom you perceive has a low value to you, he or she may relate their experience to a friend who has either a high value or a potential high value and you may lose that person as a customer too.

GOLDEN RULE

Dissatisfied customers have far more friends than satisfied ones.

The culture of your organization

Some organizations have a culture that is very much focused on the customer. Peters and Waterman talk of being 'value driven' and 'close to the customer'. In this case the organization is likely to want to make up for any shortcomings in its service almost as a matter of pride or principle.

Raffles Hotel, for example, has a reputation for elegance and excellence and feels an obligation to ensure that everything is just right for its customers. Customer recovery would, therefore, be immediate and related specifically to the customer's requirements.

Dr George R. Fath, the Vice-President of Ericsson, a communications company in the USA, says in one of his company's adverts, 'Civilization is when things work the way we expect them to', which perhaps demonstrates that getting things right for the customers is one of the core values of the business.

The view of the staff member closest to the problem

It is very likely that the staff member closest who saw or heard what happened will have a feel for what needs to be done. After all, it is likely that the staff know the customers better than, for example, the Managing Director or head office, because it is often they who are building up the relationship we talked about in the previous chapter.

For this reason, many organizations have empowered their front-line staff to deal with situations themselves and take the action they consider to be necessary to recover the situation. This often means giving them authority to offer resources or gifts. It also means encouraging them to take responsibility for their customer's problem, as we mentioned earlier. Provided the scope and limitations of that authority are clearly agreed and understood and the staff members are given full training to enable them to use their judgement on these occasions, this can be a very effective way of handling things that go wrong.

GOLDEN RULE

Unless you recover the situation quickly, a lost customer will be lost forever.

Staff who have built up a relationship with customers can feel very let down if decisions made without reference to them by a head office appear to give a lower value to the customer than they would. Such decisions may not only lose the customer but may also demotivate the staff concerned.

The more training that can be given to front-line staff, especially if it is accompanied by devolving authority, the more likely you are to gain a satisfactory outcome by building upon the staff/customer relationship. The recovery is also likely to be made at the time before any further damage is done.

Most of the organizations mentioned in this volume invest in this type of training.

As some forms of customer recovery can be expensive, it is useful for organizations to explore areas where they can give something that costs either nothing or relatively little.

A simple 'sorry' and the offer of a cup of tea might be sufficient in some cases. Often, if the staff member is seen to put him or herself out on the customer's behalf, this works wonders and is likely to involve little or no additional cost. Most customers will value this extra effort very highly.

Or the organization could keep a stock of presents that they buy in bulk from a manufacturer at low cost, which are kept almost exclusively as 'give-aways' in customer recovery. Bottles of perfume or boxes of chocolates would be examples.

Another inexpensive means is to offer up spare capacity which would otherwise have been wasted. This applies to railways or airlines, which might give free tickets or upgrades when capacity is available.

Other companies use customer recovery as a further sales opportunity. For example, they may give away a free voucher, hoping that the customer will use it as part payment for a more expensive item.

Whichever method your organization uses, you need to remember the following:

> You can possibly replace the product and this may satisfy the customer up to a point, but he or she will still have the poor product in mind.

HOWLER

A man took a key to have a copy cut at a local cobbler/ keycutter. He took it home and it didn't fit the lock. He took it back and the cutter had another try. It still didn't work. A third failure followed, after which the man asked for his money back, which he was given. At each stage, the company replaced the faulty item and finally refunded the money. But the man now goes somewhere else for such items.

In order to turn disaster to triumph, you want the customer to *forget the poor service* and *remember the recovery,* as in our Singapore Airlines example at the beginning of this chapter. If you can achieve this, you may well end up with even greater customer loyalty than before.

Let's move on to what happens if your customer recovery fails or you do not even recognize that there is a problem. In this case you are likely to receive a complaint. Or – *even worse* – no complaint.

Most people don't bother to complain. After all, there are a number of barriers that prevent people from making the effort:

- It is too much bother to sit down and write a letter.
- It might be embarrassing to ring someone up and talk to them.
- It is particularly embarrassing to complain face to face.
- Taking things back will cost extra money for bus fares etc.
- Sending things back means wrapping them up and going round to the post office or other carrier.
- The company probably won't do anything about it anyway.

THINK POINT

Think back to the last time you encountered a situation where you felt you had grounds to complain. Did you? If not, what was the reason?

In fact, whether people complain or not will usually also depend upon some of the following factors:

- How much they have paid for the product or service.
- How important it is to them.
- What they expected from it.
- The customer's background or culture.
- How many complaints they have made recently (complaint fatigue!).
- How easy or difficult the complaints procedure is.

How much they have paid for it

Clearly, people are much more likely to complain if they are dissatisfied with what they consider to be an expensive product.

How important it is to them

If the product is a vital component of the customer's own end product, then he or she is very likely to complain. In the next chapter we will be looking in more detail at customer/ supplier relationships.

What they expected from it

If the customer expected that the product would have a better performance or would last longer, he or she will be dissatisfied and will be more likely to complain. This can often apply when a company has a range of products aimed at different market segments. A customer may be drawn to the supplier by the reputation or advertising of the top-of-the-range product and assume that certain key features may apply to the lower range product.

The customer's background or culture

Whether people complain may depend upon their nationality or culture. British people, for example, have a reputation for being reluctant to complain. In such cultures the barriers to complaining will be even higher.

Complaint fatigue

Most people, even if they are prepared to complain, don't really enjoy it. If, therefore, they have come across several cases of poor service in a relatively short space of time, it is unlikely that they will take up every issue.

In addition, customers who have already complained to the same organization in the past may be reluctant to complain again, fearing that the company will regard them as professional trouble-makers.

How easy or difficult the complaints procedure is

If an organization makes the process very difficult, then it will probably receive fewer complaints. We saw the example earlier of the hospital casualty department that ran out of forms. The patient involved in that example mentioned the situation to her doctor, who told her that there were two other casualty departments within some thirty-five miles. He recommended that if she had any further accidents it was worth the extra travel to those hospitals because they had much shorter waiting times and were much more patient-orientated. The management at the first hospital know nothing about the incident because, in the end, she decided that there was no point in complaining.

So, the person who does complain has overcome all of these obstacles already and for this reason you might think that they might be:

- fairly resolute
- particularly angry
- very disappointed in the product

Let's look at these points in turn, because they are important to consider when dealing with complaints.

Fairly resolute

Well, they have got this far so there isn't much point in trying to fob them off with excuses. You need to investigate the complaint thoroughly to find out what, if anything, went wrong. If you are at fault then you need to admit it and tell them what you would like to do to put things right.

If the customer is partly to blame, you should bear in mind that if this particular person can make mistakes when using your service, then others can too. There may be a learning point for your organization. Do you need to change the instructions on the packaging, for example?

If you are not to blame at all, you still need to find some way of avoiding customers' losing face, because if they are embarrassed they are unlikely to use your product again. You might well make a simple gesture such as thanking them for giving you an opportunity to investigate the matter and giving them some encouragement to purchase again, such as a discount voucher or similar.

When the organization is in the right, this is the most dangerous time for your future relationship with that customer, and how you handle it will be crucial. It will be very easy to write a letter completely dismantling the customer's case and proving that it was their own stupid fault. In this case, you will have won a battle but you will surely lose the war!

You may feel that there are some people who either complain about everything or just 'try it on' to see what they can get out of the company. It is very likely that such people exist – some tour operators have pointed to examples of people sitting at airports writing out their complaints before they even go on their holiday. However, there are three points to bear in mind here:

1   Such people are likely to be in the minority. It takes a lot of effort to complain and most people are likely to be genuine.
2   Experience will help you to identify those who are trying it on, as will your customer database. However, you need to be aware that just because someone has already complained once about one of your products, this does not mean that a further complaint is a try on. It may well be genuine too!
3   If people feel that your organization is an easy target, as we saw in the example of the holiday complaints above, then the organization, or the industry, needs to ask itself why people feel like this. Has past performance by the organization influenced them? There is likely to be a learning point for the organization here too.

Particularly angry

Here, you will need all of your interpersonal skills. If it is a face to face complaint, you need to move to a place where you can calm things down and talk to the person in private. Offer a cup of tea. Above all, listen to what people have to say. Let them get the whole thing off their chest and show that you are listening. Active listening skills are useful here, and would include:

*   asking for clarification where appropriate
*   summarizing
*   using the appropriate body language, especially avoiding the defensive folded arms stance
*   making notes where appropriate

If the complaint is obviously justified, this would be an ideal situation for the member of staff to be empowered to offer the appropriate method of customer recovery.

If the complaint is in writing, you need to clear away from your mind the angry tone of the letter. Try to avoid becoming defensive because this is likely to be your natural reaction to someone who is angrily criticizing your organization, or your department if it is an internal customer.

Again, you need to investigate the facts because, whether the complaint is justified or not, your product has angered one person, so it could anger someone else. You need to find out what has happened and, again, learn from it.

Remember what we learned earlier, that people are usually difficult 'for a reason'. Whatever you feel personally about the complaint, you cannot deny the customer's feelings of anger or disappointment.

Very disappointed in the product

You have a customer who has expressed clear disappointment with your product. The important word here is 'expressed'. If something has gone wrong with your product, you may have a lot of other people who have clear disappointment with it. However, instead of 'expressing' it, they simply walk away and never buy again.

At least now you have a chance to put whatever is wrong right, not only for that customer but also for others who are going to be buying the product next.

In fact, what you are actually getting is *market research*. Now, some companies spend large sums on market research to find out what people like and dislike. The person who has complained is offering you this information for free. So, if you need some justification for the cost of your customer recovery, this might well be it. By acting now to put things right, you might save the company a fortune in the future. Or you may be able to design new products in a better way as a result!

There is one other thing about our complaining customer that we know. We know that he or she wants to give us another chance. Those who walk away without complaining are really saying 'Goodbye'. They are saying, 'You let me down and you won't get another chance'.

Those who complain are saying 'Hello'. They mean, 'You have let me down but I want to give you a chance to make it up to me'.

Most organizations spend a lot of time and money trying to identify customers who want to buy their products. These customers are offering themselves up for free!

GOLDEN RULE

Welcome complaints; they allow for recovery.

SUMMARY

This chapter has considered the importance of the lifetime customer, and has looked at ways of recovering customers when things have gone wrong.

6
Help, I Need Somebody; Help

PROBLEM SOLVING

In chapter 4 we saw that there were at least three dimensions to building up a relationship with your customer:

- Giving information
- Listening
- Building relationships

In this chapter we are going to look at how you can build that extra dimension, the fourth dimension. This fourth dimension involves helping your customer to solve problems and may lead to becoming part of your customer's value chain. Michael Porter writes about this in *Competitive Advantage* (1985). A value chain could be defined as 'Being an integral part of your customer's own processes'. Let's look at this in more detail.

Every organization will have features of its product that are critical to the success of that product, and which can be called vital success criteria. Kenichi Ohmae (1982) has looked at this in detail in his book *The Mind of the Strategists*, in which he talks about *key success factors*. Thus, if a supermarket intends to target those people who want their weekly shopping to be as low in cost as possible, then it will be judged on how low cost it actually is.

A supplier, therefore, that kept costs very low and worked with the supermarket to find ever more ways of keeping them that way would be in a strong position. A supplier of low cost fleet transport that was able to offer a wide-ranging distribution network between stores could work together with the supermarket to drive costs down. It may not matter too much if the fleet operator is rather inflexible, as long as the main criteria are met.

A delicatessen, on the other hand, would most likely consider its success factors to be selling a wide variety of tempting, high-quality food.

Here a supplier might have to carry a wide range of interesting food, perhaps introducing new and exciting lines at regular intervals. It may not matter if the supplies were a little more expensive.

A corner shopkeeper might see his or her vital success criteria lying in the friendliness of the staff or in the convenient hours during which the shop is open. Any internal supplier (member of staff) who can provide this friendliness is likely to be part of the value chain. If this person could also work late in the evening, he or she would be even more valuable. It may not matter particularly if this staff member was not strong enough to lift heavy boxes or crates.

An airline is likely to view safety as being very critical so it will want to work with aeroplane manufacturers who have a good record here.

An engine manufacturer might view reliability as critical, so will regard a supplier of high-quality parts as being part of the value chain. In this case there might be a wide range of vital success criteria that have to be met, such as engine performance, ease of maintenance and fuel consumption.

In order to become a part of your customer's value chain, you need to help the customer to identify what these vital success criteria are. Then, if you are able to provide solutions to these vital success criteria, you will become an integral part of the customer's own processes. The more areas in which you can offer solutions, the more important you will be in the value chain.

Looking back to Porter's five forces model, which we met in chapter 2, it will be clear that suppliers who are embedded into the value chain of their customers are in a very powerful position.

Conversely, if your organization is not part of the value chain, there are likely to be several other similar products that your customer can use, and he or she is likely to be able to switch without greatly affecting the business.

THINK POINT

Identify your own organization's vital success criteria. Can you think of any suppliers that are particularly important in helping you to achieve them?

A good example of a 'value chain would be a supplier to a manufacturing organization that operates a Just-in-Time system. You can read more about Just-in-Time in *Managing Operations* in the *In Charge* series, but here we need concern ourselves only with the principles.

In Just-in-Time operations the manufacturer keeps no stock of raw materials or assembly parts. Instead, it will have the materials delivered just as they are needed in the manufacturing process. This means that suppliers need to work to the laid-down schedule that has been agreed with the customer and supply the material exactly on schedule. This may mean that a delivery will be made every day or half day. In some cases it will mean deliveries timed to the hour.

Because the customer only has enough material to last until the agreed delivery time, if the supplier fails to deliver then the production line will stop. Because each of the separate parts of the customer's operation will also be working on a Just-in-Time basis, the next process that is supplied from this production line will also stop, until – in a very short space of time – the whole production system is at a standstill.

Not only must the delivery schedule be met, but the agreed quality must also be achieved, because any faulty material will also cause the line to stop until it is rectified.

Let's look at how the supplier fits into the customer's value chain here.

The customer's entire operation is built upon the need to reduce the holding of stock, and to have it drip fed as necessary instead.

The Just-in-Time operator is also likely to be working in a value chain with its customer and delivering the product as the customer needs it. Any fall-off in quality will lead to rejections and therefore a shortfall in the product supplied.

Therefore, tight delivery schedules and high quality can be seen as vital success criteria for the customer. The supplier that can provide this is likely to enjoy a good and profitable relationship with the customer.

Value chains can be relatively long, both internally within an organization and externally between suppliers and customers. Various materials may be supplied by a number of suppliers; they may pass through several consecutive processes within that customer organization, which may then supply the finished item as one of the inputs for its own customer's operating system. Please see the diagram in figure 15.

Clearly, the longer the value chain is, the greater opportunity there is for something to go wrong. Therefore, the closer the working relationship between the various suppliers and customers, the more effective they are likely to be.

Marks & Spencer's relationships with its suppliers can be regarded as a value chain as they are all concerned with one of the company's vital success criteria, namely quality.

In a value chain you are likely to find customers and suppliers working together to sort out problems or to bring about continuous improvements, often on a basis of sharing any of the advantages that result. They may share advances in technology, for example, or split any costs saved by a new process being introduced.

When this happens, the result is a value circle, in which providing what the customer wants brings real benefits to the supplier too. Please see the diagram in figure 16.

THINK POINT

Now identify one of your major customers. What part, if any, does your organization play in this customer's value chain?

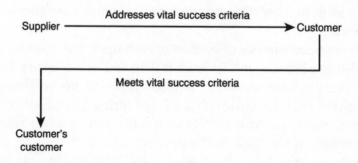

Figure 15 The value chain

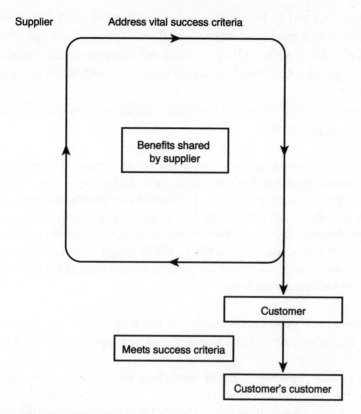

Supplier   Address vital success criteria

Benefits shared
by supplier

Customer

Meets success criteria

Customer's customer

Figure 16 The value circle

Virgin Atlantic makes good use of the value chain. One of its vital success criteria in respect of its Upper Class customers is comfort. To this end, Virgin makes use of several contractors to provide the little extras that go into making the journey as comfortable as possible. Contractors in the Virgin Atlantic Clubhouse include:

- beauty therapists (some on-flight)
- sandwich service
- shoe shiners
- hairdressers

Sarah Stoddart, of the Virgin Atlantic Clubhouse at Heathrow, stresses how important it is that all contractors have the same cultural outlook as Virgin Atlantic. They need to know as much about Virgin Atlantic as Virgin's own employees do. After all, as far as the customer is concerned, they *are* Virgin Atlantic!

It is important to be aware that value chains exist within organizations in internal customer/supplier relationships too. So there may be a long value chain within an organization, resulting in the final product, which is the one that is provided for the external customer.

Donna Griffin, Virgin Atlantic in-flight supervisor, provides a good example of this:

'There are often times when you can see that there is a problem or a potential problem for our passengers. Cabin crew are in a good position to become aware of what these problems are, either noticing them personally or being told by passengers. In some cases these problems can be addressed by action aimed at customer recovery, but in many cases the problem might involve longer term issues such as elements of the product itself that customers don't like or technical problems.'

In these cases cabin crew need to have internal suppliers in the value chain who can take these problems up for them:

'We have a monthly in-flight workshop where cabin crew can get together to discuss these issues. We can put any items on the agenda. Representatives from Product and Engineering attend and listen to what we have to say. If we make a good case and they can change things quickly, then they do. Some problems that are technical, such as light switches being in awkward places, take much longer to put right but at least we feel that someone is taking these matters up for us.

'I can ring some departments direct and often I may find that I'm talking to someone I have met in the monthly workshop so we can talk about the problem more openly. I can also refer anything to the customer services department, who I know will take it up at the appropriate level on my and my customer's behalf. Some issues will make the Top Ten list and will be discussed at Director level.

'One of the most satisfying things, though, is that we are given feedback on what has been done about the problem. We are also told why if it has been decided that things will stay as they are.

'I can give an example of an issue that I raised recently. Amenity packs were given out to children leaving Heathrow for the USA, which means that British children could use them on their holidays. American children, however, only received them at Heathrow on their way home. I was able to discuss the implications of this with the Product Department and they agreed that it should be changed.

Now, the packs are also given out in the USA and American children have them from the beginning of their holiday too.'

Clearly, the stronger the value chain within an organization, the better the final product is likely to be for the external customer. Some organizations refer to departments within their organization as 'service partners'. Others make 'service level agreements' with their internal customers, setting out in a contractual way the agreed specifications for the service that they will provide as if they were supplying external customers.

THINK POINT

Can you identify any service partners or service level agreements within your organization? If not, can you identify internal customers or suppliers with whom it would be effective to work in this way?

Let's now take a look at Home Housing, which uses both internal and external suppliers in its value chain.

We have already met the Chief Executive, Alan Kilburn, but let's look at the organization in a little more detail.

Home Housing is a housing association, which has its head-quarters in Newcastle upon Tyne but which has now expanded its operations to cover areas in the southern parts of Britain. It is split into six regions, covering different geographical areas of the country. It works in 72 local authority areas and has more than 25 000 tenancies, so it has sound claims to be considered a successful company.

Each region is empowered to run its own sphere of operations but the organization is managed at the centre by the Chief Executive, Alan Kilburn, who keeps his finger on the pulse and has that particular talent for always knowing what is going on. When asked what he would consider to be the core value of the organization, Alan will, without any hesitation, answer:

'People, we are all about people.'

There is a lot of evidence to support this.

Alan says that the important thing is to have the correct attitude and approach:

'Although we are a relatively large Association we still have the flexibility and caring attitude that you might expect from small organizations. I like to think of us as the "largest small Housing Association".'

We mentioned in chapter 4 that it is vital to value all of your customers, whether they are internal or external. Well, Home Housing takes this maxim to heart, and its 'people' policy extends to both.

THINK POINT

Would you say that your organization values people? Identify any areas where you feel that this concept would bring benefits to you or your department.

Let's look at both in turn, beginning with the external customer, who is the tenant. Home Housing uses a mix of privately raised capital and government funding (the latter currently reducing as a percentage of the total funds raised) to build homes for people to rent.

The local authority is the statutory housing authority responsible for identifying housing need and enabling the provision of new homes to meet that need. It works in partnership with a public body called the Housing Corporation to determine the allocation of central government funding for new housing schemes built by housing associations.

When making decisions about funding new housing, the Housing Corporation considers, along with other factors, the various products offered by rival housing associations. The local authority normally has the right to nominate tenants to these new housing association homes.

The end consumer, therefore, does not usually make the purchase decision directly. This decision is made by the local authority and the Housing Corporation, and is based upon a housing association's past record.

The product that Home Housing provides for the tenants includes managing the repairs and creating an atmosphere that tenants enjoy.

Clearly, 'valuing people' is very important here. The more Home Housing listens to what its tenants want, the better it is able to provide them with the services they need. This in turn is likely to influence local authorities when they make their buying decisions.

This is, therefore, an example of a value circle, as the building of relationships between tenants and housing association brings tangible benefits to both customer and supplier.

A very good example of this was when Home Housing was trying to gain support for a housing development in a local authority area in which it had not been active before. The company hired six buses and brought prospective tenants and other interested parties to view one of the existing developments so that they could see for themselves what it was like. So confident was Home Housing that everything would be found to be satisfactory that the visit was unannounced and the visitors themselves were encouraged to talk to anyone they met and to ask any questions they wanted about the company.

In the event, the visit was very successful and the high quality of the estate reflected well on Home Housing as the supplier.

Home Housing regularly carries out a tenant feedback survey covering some 2000 tenants, and is very pleased, though not complacent, about the high degree of satisfaction that they express. The most recent survey was quickly followed up with an eight-point action plan in response to service areas identifying where there was some room for improvement.

'We want our tenants to feel that we are a "good lot",' adds Alan Kilburn.

THINK POINT

How does your organization obtain feedback from its customers?

Clearly, then, one of Home Housing's vital success criteria must relate to its concern for people. It would follow, then, that in order to be part of the value chain any supplier would need to help Home Housing in this critical area.

When Home Housing wanted to establish a list of preferred suppliers to actually build new houses, it looked at what Alan Kilburn calls their 'buildability quotient'.

This means that, in addition to looking at their accounts and taking up references, Home checked each supplier out by conducting a physical inspection of their premises, looking out for orderliness on their sites, looking at how they dispose of waste etc. All of these are important if they are going to form a partner relationship with Home and help it to achieve the critical success criteria.

As far as supplying the product to the tenants is concerned, Home is very proud of its own staff who have the job of delivering on behalf of the customers. The turnover of staff is very low for the industry, and the turnover of senior managers is very low indeed, with many of them having been with the organization for many years.

Staff are encouraged to take responsibility for tenants' problems and are given training to enable them to do so.

Although the Association is very 'people' orientated and is non-profit making, it is managed as professionally as any private sector company of its size. It pays close attention to controlling costs. Alan says, 'We add value for our customers by taking a business-like approach'. He adds:

> 'The more business-like we are, the better able we are to achieve our social objectives, and the more we can value people.'

To back up this claim, Home recently came 40th out of 40 on internal costs in a survey of the leading housing associations – it spends the lowest proportion of its income on staff costs of all of these leading 40 associations! And yet it still manages to value its staff in pursuit of value to its customers.

Now that we have looked at the importance of the 'fourth dimension' and how suppliers can help their customers in the vital areas of their business, we can build this into our customer communication model, which will now look like the diagram in figure 17.

The model has now turned into a pyramid shape with a very sound foundation.

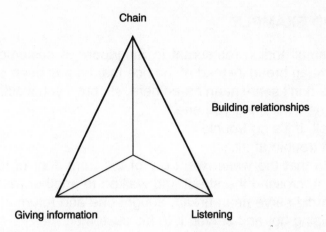

Figure 17 Four dimensions of customer communication

Let's now look at some other areas where we can help our customers.

Organizations can usually be classed culturally into two main types:

Can do

and

Can't do

Can do companies solve their customers' problems; *can't do* companies provide reasons why they can't solve their customers' problems.

The two types can be characterized by the kind of language that they use.

Can do·
- 'I'll do that straight away.'
- 'I'm sure I can arrange that. I'll ring you back in a few minutes.' (and does ring back)
- 'We can bend the rules a bit here by . . . .'
- 'We can deliver it on Thursday.'
- 'I bet one of our other branches has one in stock. I'll get them to send it to you direct.'

GOOD EXAMPLE

In a small Indian restaurant in Singapore, a customer asks for a naan bread instead of the rice that he has been offered.

'We don't serve naan bread here, sir, but if you would really like one I will bring you one.'

'Well, if it's no trouble . . . '

'No trouble at all.'

With that the waiter went out of the front door of the restaurant, crossed the street and walked to another restaurant which did serve naan bread, bought one and returned with it still piping hot and served it to his customer.

Can't do

- 'I'm a little busy at the moment. Could it wait until later?'
- 'I doubt if that will be possible. I'll ring you back later but I don't hold out much hope.'
- 'I'm afraid the rules are very strict on this point.'
- 'I'll have to check if it's in stock first, but in any case we couldn't deliver it until the end of next week.'
- 'I'm afraid we've run out.'

HOWLER

In a rather famous hotel in England at about ten o'clock in the morning, morning coffee is being served. A lady asks the waitress if she could have a sandwich with her coffee as she left home without any breakfast.

'I'm sorry madam, but we only serve biscuits with morning coffee. They are very nice and I'm sure you'll enjoy them.'

THINK POINT

Do you work for a 'can do' or a 'can't do' organization? Justify your answer with examples.

GOLDEN RULE

If you don't believe, how can you expect the customer to?

The following Howler and subsequent Good Example typify the two attitudes.

HOWLER

A couple went into a high street travel agent and tried to make a late booking. It was Saturday morning and they wanted to fly out that evening or the next day at the latest. They were prepared to go to almost any destination.

They had intended to fly out to India the previous evening but their plans had been changed at the last minute. This meant that they had a fortnight allocated which they had intended to spend abroad, they had had almost every injection that you could think of, were taking anti-malaria tablets and had sufficient money to finance a reasonably expensive holiday, although, like most people, they did want value for money.

In the high street agent, they were told how difficult it would be to find anywhere at such short notice. The date was the beginning of October. Apparently, flights would be expensive because they were not being booked in advance and packages would be difficult to find because tour operators would have given back their allocations.

The travel consultant did agree to have a go and began by telephoning an airline.

'I know this is a tall order, but I have some clients here who want to fly out tonight. I know it's unlikely that you have anything but I thought I would ring you just in case.'

Can you guess what the answer was?

Next, she tried a tour operator.

'I don't suppose you can help me and I know you have given back most of your allocations by now but . . . '

The whole time that she was occupied on the phone, she

had a hunched-up position, shook her head while talking as if willing the answer 'no', and a grimace on her face.

The couple left that agent and tried a smaller independent agent.

GOOD EXAMPLE

When the couple arrived, the agent dealt with their enquiry with a smile and telephoned a tour operator that she thought could help. She spoke to her contact positively, with a smile, and said quite simply:

'I have some clients here who would like to fly somewhere tonight, what can you offer them?'

She did not find it easy to arrange a deal and it took some two hours of telephoning back and forth, but a holiday was found, not for that evening but departing the next day, and the couple left the shop happy with a booking for a fortnight in the Seychelles.

From the very outset, with her attitude, her actions, her manner and her body language she had conveyed to the clients *and*, more importantly, to the operator that she intended to succeed – and she did.

And now let's look at another can't do organization:

HOWLER

A couple go to the travel desk in a hotel in Cairns, Australia. They want to book a seaplane to take them to an island on the Great Barrier Reef. The assistant shakes her head and says, 'We usually have to have several people to fill the plane. I'm sure they won't just accept two of you.'

'Well, could you try, please?'

The assistant telephoned the company but the line was engaged and she suggested that they call back later and she would tell them whether she had been able to arrange it.

When they called back she was apologetic and explained

that the only hope of arranging a trip was if at least another two people came forward for the trip to make it worth their while flying the plane. If two other people did enquire she would let them know.

The couple were very disappointed. They decided to ring the number that they had seen on the brochure direct. They were told that there was no problem in arranging a flight for just the two of them and they could fly out tomorrow if they wished.

They did, and they had a fantastic time!

Let's assume that you work for a 'can do' organization. It is important to structure your approach to solving your customers' problems. Let's now look at a seven-step approach:

1 Make sure you know what the problem is.
2 Analyse the situation carefully.
3 Develop options.
4 Select the way forward.
5 Agree a delivery schedule.
6 Ensure that the customer knows how the product works.
7 Check that your customer is receiving the benefits from the solution.

We can now look at each of these steps in more detail and consider how they work in practice.

1 Make sure you know what the problem is

This may seem an obvious point but it is probably the most important step in the whole process. We may think that we know what the problem is, but we often miss the real problem and only address a symptom. So how do you find out what the problem is?

You need to gather as much relevant information as you can.

The first, most obvious, step is to ask your customer. This may mean carrying out some market research. The Top Ten list of Virgin Atlantic Airlines is a good example here. Virgin uses feedback forms and complaints to find out if there are any problems, and the Top Ten to highlight the real issues that concern a lot of customers. Once the company knows what these issues are, they can be addressed.

Home Housing carries out regular feedback exercises so it can find out what really concerns the tenants.

It is important to note that it is just as important to carry out this step with your internal customers as it is with external ones. Many managers, for example, are supplied with regular information by the other departments of the organization. Often, they receive what that department thinks they ought to receive or what they find easy to produce rather than what the managers actually need to run the business.

If the business managers of the company meet representatives from the other department and explore what the important areas are, then information can be provided that will target these areas. The supplying department will then be helping the business managers to meet their vital success criteria, and can then be considered to be part of the internal value chain.

This point is particularly important during the installation of management information systems. It is vital that the people who are going to use such systems are asked what they want from them.

HOWLER

Several managers from the same company were attending a management seminar. They were asked to describe the products that their departments provided for internal customers. A member of the Finance Department explained that she produced figures on a monthly basis to show how much was spent on overtime.

'Why can't you give us those figures on a weekly basis? They would be much more useful.'

'We can do that if you want; in fact, it's easier for us! No one has ever asked us for that before.'

'We didn't know we could ask! Perhaps we should sit down together and discuss what we need and how you can help!'

'Good idea!'

GOLDEN RULE

You must listen to your customers to find out what they want.

You might not always be able to find out the problem from the customer. You may need to analyse trends and use statistical information to help you. After all, the customers may not even know that they have a problem.

In this case, you might offer to test something on their behalf to see if there is a problem. For example, opticians offer eye tests to see if there is anything wrong, while garages offer to carry out checks on your car.

During this first stage you need to ask a lot of open questions to really find out what the current situation is. Typical questions will begin with:

- Who . . . ?
- What . . . ?
- Where . . . ?
- When . . . ?
- How . . . ?

Let's suppose your company sells a range of office equipment, including personal computers, photocopiers, scanners etc.

A customer rings you up and says that she feels the need to replace her current photocopier, which is used by everyone in the office. It is not processing quickly enough and queues are building up around it, with a resulting loss in productivity.

You might simply discuss a range of photocopiers with her and agree to provide one that meets her requirements and is in the right price range.

Or you might enter into the first stage of the seven-step process.

You could talk to her and try to find out what the real problem is. You might find that there is only one copier for the building. Perhaps each department needs to make only half a dozen copies, but they all need it at the same time.

You could use open questions:

- Who uses it?

'Every department has some use for it at some time of the day. However, the personnel department is the heaviest user – in fact, it accounts for 60 per cent of all copies. On the other hand, the finance department use it relatively little.'

- When is the period of most demand?

'Demand appears to be even throughout the day, with a lull during the lunch break. There is a small peak just before four o'clock as people remember they have to catch the post.'

- What other equipment do they have?

'Most departments have at least one small computer, though they are not linked in a network.'

- Where are most of the copies sent?

'It seems that most are for internal use, though some are sent externally.'

- Where is the copier located?

'In a room on the other side of the building from the personnel department, in fact next door to the finance department, who use it least.'

These are only examples of the types of answer you might receive during your information gathering. Once you are satisfied that you have the information, you can move on to the second stage of the process.

2 Analyse the situation carefully

In stage 1 you found out what is happening. Now you need to find out why things happen and whether they could be done differently. During this stage you are likely to use questions such as:

- Why ... ?
- What if ... ?

So let's ask some more questions:

- Why do people need so many hard copies?

'Most people are taking off several copies of letters or forms to send round to other departments. Usually they take off more than they need because if they find they need more it is a real hassle to come back and queue again. This seems to be compounding the problem.'

- What if copies were not available?

'We wouldn't be able to exchange information with other departments to keep them in the picture.'

- What if the copies being sent around were not hard copies?

'Well that would be OK for most departments but not for personnel who need to keep information on personal files.'

- Why do they need to be physical files? Could they be kept on computer discs with a safe back-up system?

'Perhaps.'

- As there seem to be different requirements in the various departments, would you consider more than one solution?

'I see what you mean. We could treat personnel as a different problem.'

You are now beginning to develop options, the third step in the process.

3 Develop options

Now that you have enough information to identify the problem and the issues surrounding it, you can begin to look for solutions. There are likely to be several alternatives. Each may have advantages and disadvantages. You and your customer need to test these options to see which provides the best solution.

- What if the various computers were linked to each other so that people could pass information around by electronic mail?

'Well, that would be OK and it would also help our communications within the office, which are not really very good at the moment. I'm still a little concerned about not having hard copies for the personnel department, though.'

- What if personnel had their own smaller copier in their department and everyone was linked by email?

'Hm ... the other departments will still need to do some photocopying.'

- What if they had access to a small scanner? It will do small photocopying jobs and it will give them greater flexibility. They will be able to scan in documents that they haven't written but that they would like to keep in their computer file.

'Oh, we've been thinking about scanners for a while now, but I hadn't realized that they could be used as a photocopier too.'

There may be several other options, but you are nearing a position where you can move on to the fourth stage.

4 Select the way forward

Now you can help your customer to select the best option from those that you have identified. You need to remember at this stage that the optimum solution is likely to be that which best addresses the vital success criteria upon which the customer will be judged.

You may also come up with brilliantly new innovative solutions, which will help you and your customer to stay one step ahead of the competition. We will look at this in a little more detail later.

Let's go back to our example:

'I think we have a possible solution here. We'll introduce electronic mail, install a smaller photocopier in the personnel department and then assess which departments might benefit from a scanner. When I think about it, the important thing for personnel is the record keeping aspect, which is why we want to have hard copies but the really important issue for the other departments is communication, and this will bring us enormous benefits here.'

You have begun to identify a way forward here which fits in with the vital success criteria, which turns out to be – *communication*.

Now that you have identified a way forward, you need to deliver it, which is the fifth stage.

5 Agree a delivery schedule

It is important that whenever you agree to supply your customer, both parties have a clear understanding of when it will be delivered. In some cases, this will be agreed immediately after the solution has been identified. In others it might be set in advance, and the solution and delivery must be within a set deadline.

For example, let's suppose a car manufacturer has asked its supplier of car seats to strengthen them to make them safer in an accident. There will be a deadline within which the solution must be designed and produced so that it can fit in with the production of the model for which it is being manufactured.

In fact, when a customer is looking for suppliers, it may well be that stage 5, delivery, is so crucial that it is one of the vital success criteria. In this case it may well become stage 1 in the six-step process.

Once you have agreed the schedule, meet it!

The following stage is one that is often overlooked. Your responsibility to your customer does not end with delivery of the product or service. You need to be sure that the customer knows how to use it!

6 Ensure that the customer knows how the product works

In chapter 5 we discussed the need for clear instructions. In many cases, instructions will not be sufficient and they will have to be supplemented by a demonstration or initial training of staff on how to use the product. Whether this comes as a part of the product or is carried out at additional cost needs to be specified clearly when agreeing the terms and price in any contract.

You may also want to offer some kind of after-sales service to ensure that if anything does go wrong your customer turns to you for help and not to one of your competitors.

The most successful products are likely to be those that the customer finds easy to use. A good example of this is the personal computer. In the early days of their development, PCs were not particularly user friendly, and the user had to learn a sophisticated language to be able to gain any benefit from them. Now, computers are relatively easy to operate and the most successful software packages come with instructions, not only in a manual but also on screen, and if all else fails they are often backed up with a user helpline.

HOWLER

A man hires a car in the USA. He drives from the parking lot to his hotel, some thirty miles away. He turns off the ignition and tries to remove the key. It won't budge! He looks in the glove compartment and there is no owner's handbook or any manual of any kind.

The same key also locks the doors and boot of the car. If the car is left unlocked and is subsequently stolen, he will have contravened his hire agreement and will be liable to pay for the car.

So he cannot leave the car without removing the key from the ignition. He has another try. He is beginning to be creative and twists it now quickly, now slowly. He even creeps slyly up on it and tries to wrest it out before it has a chance to realize that he is trying to remove it!

All to no avail.

He leaves the car and goes into the hotel reception area. He rings the car hire company. They don't know what to do so they give him the phone number of a local mechanic who does some maintenance work for them.

The mechanic's wife says that he will be home in about thirty minutes and she will get him to ring the hotel as soon as he arrives.

The man thanks her and sits in the hotel reception with one eye on his suitcase and one eye on the car in the car park.

After about twenty minutes the mechanic rings. 'Ah, yes, you have to follow a particular sequence on that model. Didn't anybody tell you? Here's how you do it . . . '

Now that you have reached the sixth stage, your customer is using the product and you might feel that this is the end of the process. However, there is one more stage.

7 Check that your customer is receiving the benefits from the solution

It is very important that you monitor the results of the solution and discuss them with your customer. This allows you to take any corrective action that may be necessary. It also means that it is you who is on hand when the next problem arises rather than one of your competitors, so it is to you that the customer is likely to turn for help in solving it.

GOLDEN RULE

If you don't look after your customers, somebody else will.

So far in this chapter we have looked at solving problems, and this can be a very powerful way of building up your relationship with your customer. However, there is one particularly important aspect that we should mention.

Some organizations imply that there are problems when there aren't any, but they worry the customer enough so that they buy the solution recommended by the organization.

This is unlikely to lead to a good long-term relationship, although it might bring in one sale before the customer realizes what has happened

HOWLER

A couple check in at a car hire desk to pick up a car that they have reserved and paid for in advance. As they are filling in the forms, the counter assistant asks them whether they want to pay extra to upgrade the car to a bigger model, 'Because the one you've booked is pretty small and could be uncomfortable. I would strongly advise you to go for the upgrade.'

The car is located some distance from the counter and is not visible to them.

The couple think for a moment but decide against it, as they have only a very small amount of luggage and there is only the two of them. And they've already spent more than they really wanted to.

When they reach the car, they find it to be perfectly adequate for their needs and conclude that the hire company simply wanted to make as much out of the deal as possible.

They don't use that company any more!

GOLDEN RULE

Dissatisfied customers have far more friends than satisfied ones.

We mentioned earlier that you might be able to produce a highly innovative solution for your customer. As technological advances accelerate and customers' tastes and requirements change, there is a need for organizations to be ever more innovative.

It is often very difficult to look ahead to see what is going to be available or needed several years in advance. Some organizations, however, must look many years in advance if they are going to stay in business. The development of the new large aircraft being considered by both Boeing and Airbus is a good example.

Airlines have foreseen a need for a completely different type of aeroplane for the 21st century. Possibilities being considered are that the new aeroplane might have a bar, a cinema and lounge areas, which is light years away from the current concept of sitting for many hours immobile in your seat.

The world changes all of the time and each morning when we wake up, millions of things will be different from when we woke up yesterday. And the pace of change is accelerating!

Most people find it very difficult to try to imagine what things will look like in two or three years' time, and impossible to imagine ten years hence. Asking people to think of things any further ahead than that is likely to result in them coming up with a mental block, much the same as if you asked them to picture how big the universe is.

In fact, we can use space travel as a good example. The first manned flight took place in 1903, culminating in the first manned moon landing in 1969.

Once the moon was reached there was the inevitable anticlimax of 'now that we're there, what can we do with it?'. Subsequent space projects have had to be justified on a commercial basis using the space shuttle and interest has waned as space flight has apparently become more routine.

Unmanned flights have been sent off to explore the outer limits of the solar system and have raised some excitement, but there has always been the barrier that the universe is so big that it would take far too long to reach anywhere that might be inhabitable.

Until now ... scientists are now exploring the possibility that it may be possible to design space craft capable of approaching the speed of light, reducing the journey to Mars from one year to one month!

At the same time, eminent scientists are even advancing the theory that it may be possible to travel through time itself!

It may not be long before we only need say, 'Beam me up Scotty', as they do in *Star Trek*!

Similar advances have been made in the world of medicine. In the early 1960s, the first, relatively unsuccessful, heart transplants were carried out. Now for the first time a man has been fitted with a permanent electric heart.

The introduction of the plastic card has done the same for handling money. Soon we may have only one card, which serves a wide variety of purposes, from allowing us to spend or transfer money to opening our own front door. It may serve as a passport or tell you when your next dental check-up is due. It is only relatively recently that we had to take our cheque books to the superstore!

Many of these advances are made in response to identified customer needs. Housing Associations brought in a very innovative solution for people who could not afford to buy their homes completely, and offered a scheme in which customers bought half of it and rented the other half until such time as they were in a position to buy it. This was a very innovative solution at the time.

However, some innovations are made in areas where people didn't even know they had a need. Satellite TV is a good example of this, and so is the personal computer.

Whatever field of activity your organization is in, you need to be aware of the need for innovation to stay ahead of your competition and to satisfy your customers' ever-changing tastes. The world out there is not standing still, and you can't afford to stand still either. We will look at change in more detail in the next chapter.

SUMMARY

In this chapter we have considered the value chain concept and looked at the importance of solving your customers' problems.

7
The Times They Are A-Changin'

THE MANAGEMENT AND OWNERSHIP OF CHANGE

Life is not constant. Very few things remain unchanged for long. We have only to look at the advances in communications technology in the past few years to realize how fast and how significant the changes have been.

While we may often yearn for change, when it comes we are not so sure. Perhaps what we had before wasn't so bad after all – we did 'know' it. What the new situation will be is somewhat unknown.

This, indeed, is part of the theory behind the comfort zone concept postulated by Tice, which is considered later in this chapter. Even though it may not be a perfect situation, we are comfortable with what we know and may be reluctant to change even though we are promised that things will be better.

Innovation has already been shown to be an important part of customer satisfaction, in the previous chapter. This chapter looks at the ways in which people react to change and the implications these have for customers. Having considered the Product Life Cycle and Organizational Body Language in earlier chapters, you will be introduced to the concept of the *Organizational Life Cycle* and the ways in which the organization itself adapts to change and the implications these have for customer satisfaction.

It might be presumed that all changes will be beneficial for the customer – and, indeed, many are – but, as we shall consider, change, even change for the better, can be uncomfortable, thus those involved with customer satisfaction need to understand the psychology of the change process.

Lou Tice of the Pacific Institute in Seattle, Washington has worked on the concept of 'comfort zones'.

Basically, Tice postulates that we all live and work in zones in which we are comfortable and that we will tend to resist changes that move us out of these zones, whether the change is for the better or the worse. We can all understand a reluctance to move to a worse situation, but you may have problems believing that there will be resistance to a move for the better. There is plenty of evidence that the winners of large sums of money through lotteries, football pools, Premium Bonds and other forms of easy access gambling become very uncomfortable with their new-found wealth, and in extreme cases they may spend so freely that they are soon back where they started from. Such winners need considerable help and support in order to adapt to their new situation and thus to establish a new comfort zone. In the USA, there is the concept of 'buyer's regret' (introduced in chapter 1), whereby a customer who has purchased a product begins to have second thoughts soon after the purchase. Where delivery is not immediate, e.g. a new vehicle, there is a considerable temptation to cancel the order and to stay with what one knows. Psychologically it is perhaps better to stay with what one knows, even if it is far from perfect, than to move to something else which may be better – but life teaches us that one can never be sure that things will turn out exactly as planned.

THINK POINT

Can you think of occasions where you have suffered from buyer's regret?

The comfort zones concept has tremendous implications for all of those involved with customer satisfaction. You may be fully convinced of the benefits of a new product or service but the customer may be reluctant. Advertisers overcome this problem by 'thinking through', i.e. showing the potential user what life will be like when using the product or service, thus bypassing any discomfort of the actual changes involved. Even minor changes, e.g. packaging, can provide a short-term degree of discomfort for the customer, thus it is important that you not only

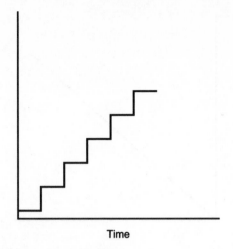

Time

Figure 18 Incremental change

stress the benefits but encourage the customer to concentrate on how life will be once he or she is using the product or service. It is only the process of change that provides the discomfort, not the end result. Even when the end result is not a better one, human resilience becomes used to it. We can cope with disabilities, changed circumstances – the problems lie in the transition period. These problems have been modelled by Kurt Lewin as follows.

Kurt Lewin (1951), an American, has developed an interesting way of looking at change, that many supervisors/first-line managers have found extremely useful when required to implement organizational changes.

Lewin's concept was that although *change* can often be planned, the outcome is never certain. Were change incremental (in small, planned steps), as shown in figure 18, or smooth, as shown in figure 19, then life would be simple – changes would be small and non-threatening.

However, the reality is more like figure 20.

Real change, i.e. change in the real world, involves rapid movement from a stable position to a new position, which then stabilizes before the next rapid movement. The reasons for the change are often external and may include product changes, legislation and economic factors. The sudden movement from a stable position can be very threatening. The concept is that the stable position must first be broken up into an unstructured amorphous one, and that it will then reform into a new position; the difficulty is that it is impossible to predict with a great deal of accuracy the

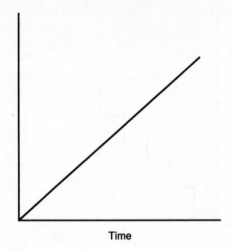

Time

Figure 19 Smooth change

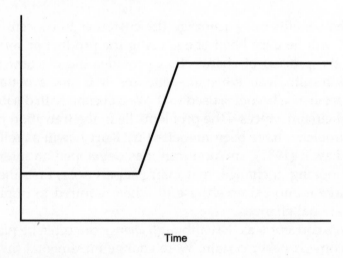

Time

Figure 20 Real change

exact form of the new position. As the airframe manufacturers found, the advent of the first commercially successful jet airliner, the Boeing 707 as opposed to the Comet 1 (see chapter 2), led to the complete demise of propeller-driven models, and the competition had a very difficult job catching up with Boeing. This was a massive change. Indeed, transportation and telecommunications have seen the biggest and swiftest changes in history. In less than one century we have gone from the men making a short flight at Kitty Hawk (the Wright brothers) to men reaching the moon – change does not come any more dramatic than this!

Lewin talked about being frozen into a position, unfreezing,

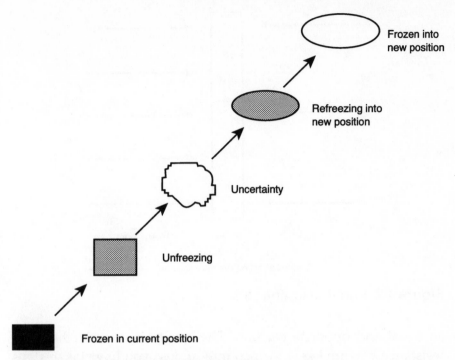

Frozen into
new position

Refreezing into
new position

Uncertainty

Unfreezing

Frozen in current position

Figure 21 Unfreezing and refreezing

the uncertainty that this produces, refreezing into a new position and then being frozen into the new position. This can be illustrated diagrammatically as in figure 21.

Lewin then produced his 'Force Field Analysis' approach for dealing with changes.

If you examine the way in which people try to implement change, they often try to overcome any resistance by pushing harder.

THINK POINT

This is a Think Point that requires some physical action. Ask somebody to hold out their hand to you with their palm at right angles to their arm. You do the same and place your palm over theirs and push (gently!). What do they do? In all probability, they will push back.

Newton's Third Law of Motion is that for every action there is

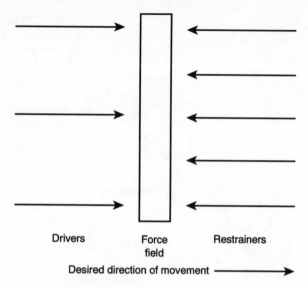

Figure 22 Force field analysis

an equal and opposite reaction. The harder you push, the more resistance you are likely to encounter unless you have taken steps to reduce the resistance. This can be illustrated as in figure 22.

The Lewin technique suggests that you consider all of the reasons for making a change – the *drivers* – and then all those reasons for holding back – the *restrainers*. You can even make them of different lengths and thicknesses on your diagram to reflect different priorities and anxieties. If, taking all factors into consideration, the restrainers outnumber the drivers, change will be uncomfortable, may have damaging effects on relationships and will require considerable energy. If, on the other hand, you can look at the restrainers and come up with strategies to remove fears and anxieties, then the change will occur with relatively less disruption and will need less energy. Thus, the more you push customers to accept changes, the more likely they are to dig in and resist you; you need to work with them to overcome their resistance to the changes.

In order to carry out this analysis with success, you will need to know a little about the psychological reactions to change that people, including yourself, go through.

The 'Coping Cycle' of Adams, Hayes and Hopson (1976) suggests that we go through five stages in our reaction and coming to terms with change:

1 Denial
2 Defence
3 Discarding
4 Adaptation
5 Internalization

Although originally postulated with the needs of organizations in mind, the cycle is equally relevant to personal change.

Stage 1: Denial

As is often said, 'I don't know why they want to change things around anyway'. One of the first reactions to change, after the idea has had time to sink in, is to deny that there is any need for it. In the terms of Lewin and Tice, we are comfortable in the position we are in; we may well not wish to acknowledge the need to unfreeze. Note the use of the word 'acknowledge'; we may know full well that change is necessary but we do not want to admit that it is, or if we do admit it then we might not want it to go so far or in a particular direction.

Stage 2: Defence

Change means that life is going to be different. You may find yourself having to deal with new people, new ideas, new technologies, a new location etc. Even when you admit that the change is necessary and acknowledge it publicly, defence still occurs. You will want to maintain as much of your comfort zone as possible. Perhaps change can be just the same only better! Because you know that it is necessary and that your defence is more instinctive than rational, self-esteem can go down. You know it's a losing battle but you feel that you have to fight it. Don't worry: it's a natural part of the cycle, because it leads on to the third stage.

Stage 3: Discarding

Two things begin to happen. First, as you refreeze into the new situation you begin to become more comfortable with it and, secondly, because of this, you can begin to discard any of the old ideas you had that were acting as restrainers. An example of this can be seen when people move to another part of the country.

First, they try to keep up with their old friends and may not socialize much, but then they begin to discard those acquaintances who were not especially close and make new ones in the new location. Eventually they move to Stage 4, adaptation, where their lives are adapted to keep the best of the old while becoming comfortable in the new.

Stage 4: Adaptation

As mentioned above, we don't discard everything from before. We adapt the best and fit it into our new situation, a situation that we have become frozen into, and that leads to the final stage.

Stage 5: Internalization

When the change started, the old situation was what you were comfortable with and the new was threatening. By the time you have been through the first four stages, you have reached a point where it is the new situation that you are comfortable with: you have internalized it; it is part of you. People who return to an area after a number of years or back to a firm they were happy with are often surprised to find how uncomfortable they are; they are no longer in their comfort zone.

If we examine this through a simple analogy, we can see how the mechanism works.

A couple have a seven-year-old washing machine. It still works but newer machines are more efficient and have enhanced features. While wandering around their local electrical store one Saturday, they fall into conversation with a salesperson who tries to convince them that they should trade their machine in for a newer one.

Firstly, they deny the need to change, Stage 1:

- It still works OK.
- We're used to its little idiosyncrasies.
- We have better things to spend our money on.

If the salesperson gives up at this stage there will be no sale, but remember, this is only Stage 1. Stage 2 is defence, and it adds a little more to the thought processes:

- We probably do need a new machine but we don't need a salesperson to tell us.
- We'll make a decision in our own time.
- If we're going to buy a new one, we need time to think about it.

There is movement, but not a great deal. However, if we can move them to Stage 3, they begin to discard their old ideas:

- You know, these machines are much more efficient.
- A new machine would be more environmentally friendly.
- (and even) I'm fed up with my friends telling me what their machines can do.

The couple are now actively switched on to the idea of a new machine and may start talking in Stage 4 (adaptation) language:

- It'll fit nicely where the old one is.
- It does the washing more quickly so we'll have more time for other things.
- If we don't buy now, the prices will probably rise.

The chances are they will buy the machine and when they have it at home, they will use the language of Stage 5, internalization:

- I don't know how we managed with that old machine; this one is much better!

This book does not intend to be a treatise on selling but many of the techniques of selling are rooted in a knowledge of the psychology of change.

From the salesperson's point of view, there are two issues:

1 They may place the order, go home and suffer from buyer's regret, with the danger of cancellation, or
2 In five to seven years' time the whole process will need to be repeated from Stage 1 again – that's the nature of change.

Whatever changes you decide to make to your life or whatever changes are imposed on you at work or at home, there will be some discomfort. Not all changes will lead to better conditions: illness or work changes may lead to a considerable change of lifestyle. What you and your customer need to do is to think through the uncomfortable experience of the change itself and start to plan for the new position.

These concepts work whether you are a salesperson selling a new product that brings positive benefits or a medical practitioner giving a patient bad news: it is the uncertainty of change that produces stress; the end result most people can internalize and create a new comfort zone.

Ken Bogas is a restaurateur in Vancouver, British Columbia. Having been in the business for a number of years, he has instituted a dramatic conceptual change at his restaurant, 'Mangiamo'. The restaurant is popular with business people and with local sports stars. Whereas in other similar establishments there is a clear divide between the food preparation areas and the customers, not so at Mangiamo. Normally, the more exclusive and expensive the establishment, the more what happens behind the scenes is hidden. One of the great charms of the New York diners and the British fish and chip shops is that you can often see your food being prepared and even talk to the staff preparing it. By introducing the radical change of removing the partitions between customers and the kitchens, and even providing a bar for customers to sit and eat at that is directly linked to the kitchen area, Ken allows his customers – over 200 of them on a busy night – to interact with the staff directly. Ken sees this close link between customers, staff and the product as a key factor in the success of the establishment, which has had very good reviews in the Canadian press, and the customers seem to love it. The opening up of hitherto forbidden areas has given customers a new respect for the kitchens and has provided an opportunity for all of the staff to relate to the end user and not just the waiters and bus boys as in more traditional restaurant arrangements. This has required the recruitment of staff who can deal with the change to direct contact with customers, and Ken needs to give considerable direction to ensure that the establishment is functioning as perfectly as possible. With the kitchen opened up, errors can be seen more easily. Ken Bogas demonstrates one of the great tenets of quality: if you make your operation transparent, the customer can see exactly what is going on and thus quality standards need to be the highest possible. Equally, Ken's customers, because they are invited to be involved, are very loyal. By virtue of the layout of Mangiamo, you are more than a customer and from the staff point of view more than an employee; the changes Ken has instituted make you a part of the organization.

THINK POINT

How aware are your customers of what goes on behind the scenes? Are they encouraged or discouraged from seeing the way your products or services are put together? Are your behind the scenes staff encouraged to meet the customers?

It can be very useful for those who put the product or service together to meet the end user; that way, customer wants and needs become known directly. Remember:

GOLDEN RULE

You must listen to your customers to find out what they want.

Even when you have an improved product or service and you wish to encourage your customers to purchase it, you must make sure that you have thought through all of the implications for systems, organizational structure and training that it will require, otherwise problems can occur.

HOWLER

A postal delivery organization introduced a new service that, for a small payment, held a customers' mail while they were on holiday etc. The idea was to assist the fight against burglaries by ensuring that there was not a tell-tale build up of mail to show that the house was empty.

One customer found that on three out of the four occasions when he used the service, mail was actually delivered. Although a refund of the fee was made on each occasion,

> the customer came to distrust the ability of the supplier and felt that the security of his home had been threatened. For this to happen on three out of four occasions suggests that the systems to support what was an excellent idea were not in place and thus the supposed change for the better was negated.

For some, changes happen more regularly than for others. For the singer, Jill Galt, there is a constant need to ensure that her repertoire includes the latest songs as well as old favourites. Our wish to hear such old favourites is another example of comfort zones in operation. Mark Bryant, the librarian whom we considered in chapter 2, has been involved in considerable changes in the Buckinghamshire library service, changes designed to meet the evolving needs of customers and the way they use their leisure time.

Libraries used to be about books, then came the use of on-line and off-line databases to search for books and articles. Mark now considers that customers require videos and CDs on a loan basis. True, there are problems, not least with costs, but the introduction of such services, developed through customer comments, has led to a library provision in Buckinghamshire that fulfils many of the criteria of excellence and innovation we have considered in previous chapters.

Andrew Gibson is a general practitioner, providing medical services on a new housing estate in the South Midlands of the UK. His surgery is a Portacabin while he awaits a purpose-built facility. He too has introduced changes and has removed many of the barriers that have existed between doctors and their staff and patients, now customers. The introduction of customer service has followed the concept of budget holding in the UK National Health Service. Dr Gibson's reception staff are helpful and try to please where possible. He has arrangements with local medicine dispensaries so that patients do not have to go to the surgery, pick up a prescription and then visit the pharmacy; repeat prescriptions can be sent directly to the pharmacy or medicines can be collected from the surgery in special cases. The estate contains families who are likely to have vacations abroad, therefore there is a travel advice unit as well as the facility for vaccinations and information. Andrew Gibson is not unique, but he serves to illustrate the growth in effective customer service that has developed within the UK publicly funded health service over the past few years – changes that make the patients feel like genuine customers and not numbers on a list.

In November 1995, the Business and Technology Education Council (BTEC), one of the major qualification awarding bodies in the UK, introduced a computerized report system for its external verifiers. BTEC validates courses for universities, colleges, schools and private providers on an increasingly international basis. Both of the authors have worked on BTEC-validated programmes in the UK, India, the Netherlands and the USA, and with students worldwide. In order to ensure quality, BTEC employs part-time external verifiers, who visit programme providers and report on quality and assessment issues. Reports used to be in ballpoint on NCR (no carbon required) sheets, one for the centre providing the programme, one for the BTEC regional manager, one for BTEC HQ and one for the external verifier. The writing on the last sheet was often very feint indeed. The new system uses a hard disk database with all of the verifier's and centre's details included, which allows for word processing and archiving. This eases the task of the external verifier, who in this case is the internal customer, and provides a better and more professional service to the external customer, the centre providing the programme. There are a number of awarding bodies in the UK, thus BTEC is in a competitive situation and has responded by changing systems so that there is an overall benefit: added value, in the language of earlier chapters.

THINK POINT

What changes has your organization instituted in the past year that benefit both internal and external customers?

In the 1960s, as Irving (1993) has described, the first of the wide-bodied 'Jumbo Jets', the Boeing 747, was developed, not only by Boeing but with considerable input from Pan Am, the launch customer. This degree of involvement is becoming the norm rather than the exception. Food manufacturers, supermarkets and domestic appliance manufacturers all use customer panels to assist them in the change process. Dr Gibson, mentioned earlier, has consulted patients about their requirements for his new surgery – after all, it will be their surgery too.

HOWLER

In the late 1940s, a major automobile manufacturer introduced a model that encompassed all of the technological changes that the designers thought the customers would want – but they didn't, and the car was soon withdrawn from the market. You must involve your customers in the change process wherever possible.

Throughout this book, there have been examples of organizations and individuals making changes that benefit their customers, and in doing so increasing their market share: P&O introducing the *Oriana*, a superliner for the UK market, Bill Shepard offering advice and signed books, libraries with CDs etc. available. What we now need to consider is the changes that organizations undergo and the effects that these will have on their customers.

Organizations can undergo a life cycle similar to that for products – and, indeed, similar to that for human beings. If we use a diagram similar to that for the product life cycle (chapter 2), we can use different language to describe the stages. For the Organizational Life Cycle (figure 23), we will use the terms:

- Birth
- Adolescence
- Maturity
- Menopause
- Decline

We hope that changes at the menopausal stage result in decline being averted and the organization gaining a new, albeit different, lease of life.

Let's look at each of these in turn and relate any problems that may occur to the LICAL (Lying, Ignorance, Complacency, Arrogance, Lethargy) concept introduced in chapter 1.

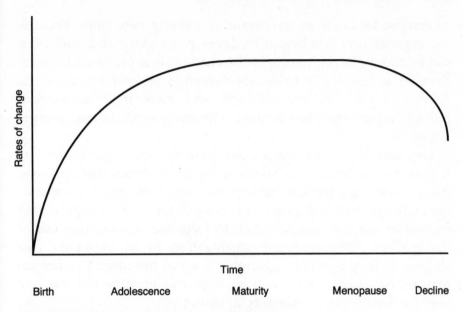

Figure 23 axis labels: Rates of change (y-axis), Time (x-axis), Birth, Adolescence, Maturity, Menopause, Decline

Figure 23 The organizational life cycle

Birth

At this stage, the organization is new and keen to gain customers. There may be launch offers, and prices may be kept low in an attempt to gain market share. The dangers are lying, i.e. promising that which you know cannot be delivered, and ignorance. A new company may be relatively naive but may well be dealing with sophisticated customers. Customers are likely to be new and the gaining of further new customers is all-important. Such an organization can change very rapidly but may attempt changes that are beyond its resources. This can be compounded by the customers demanding more and more in an attempt to gain greater value for less cost. An organization that wishes to survive into adolescence needs to realize which changes it can encompass and which it cannot. When looking at the rates of change, they are likely to be high and positive. By positive, we mean likely to enhance customer satisfaction.

Adolescence

The adolescent organization is gaining both in confidence and sophistication. Competitors may see it as a growing force. The customer base will be growing and the keeping of repeat customers becomes as important as gaining new ones. Because the organization has begun to develop a history and culture, it can be more discriminating in the changes it is prepared to introduce. It is less likely to accept demands beyond its resources. Arrogance can become a danger and there may be residual naiveté, especially when dealing with more sophisticated competition.

This can be a very dangerous time for the organization, as it may be vulnerable to takeover by more established players. Adolescent organizations often have cash flow problems associated with growth and a cash-rich competitor may attempt to gain control or use the cash situation to force the organization out of the market. An adolescent organization in an oligopoly (see chapter 2) may be very vulnerable if all of the other players are mature. Rates of change will be high and positive but the rate may be decreasing as maturity approaches.

Maturity

Maturity is the time of greatest stability, and thus a time when the organization may not want to make changes unless they are forced upon it. Markets are known and there is a strong customer base. Arrogance and complacency are the biggest dangers. The organization resents newcomers and yet, paradoxically, may take its customers for granted and be reluctant to accept the changes they require. Rates of change will be low and moving from positive towards neutral, i.e. they will not positively add to customer satisfaction.

Menopause

Dr Miriam Stoppard (1980) says of menopause that it may cause no problems at all or, at its extreme, be characterized by hot flushes, tearfulness, anxiety, profound depression, inability to concentrate, inability to deal with problems and inability to make decisions. Biologically, menopause is a condition built into the endocrine (hormonal) system of the body and that it will occur is inevitable; it is known in Western society as 'The Change'. It is not necessarily a change for the worse, although while the hormonal changes are occurring, the concepts of comfort zones and freezing that we looked at earlier in this chapter may apply. It is not within our remit to consider the male menopause or the social implications of menopause etc.; we just wish to use a natural part of the human life cycle to aid understanding of organizational behaviour.

Many find that they acquire new interests after menopause.

We believe that there is a menopausal stage in many organizations, where, after a period of relative maturity, outside forces cause alterations in markets, available technologies, and customer requirements and perceptions. Just like hormones in the body, the organization cannot control these forces, and this may bring about inabilities in decision making, failure to deal with problems, organization anxiety and depression. If you have ever worked in such an organization, you may recognize the organizational 'hot flush' that seems to affect the entire workforce from time to time. The organization becomes more interested in its problems than those of the customers, and any changes tend to be inwardly focused on systems and, especially, organizational structures rather than on the products, services and customers. Lethargy becomes a danger – a paradoxical danger, because lethargy is what will destroy the organization and yet, just when the organization needs to concentrate on its position and survival, it becomes lethargic. The main dangers are ultimate decline following a loss of customer base or else a takeover by a competitor. Indeed, menopausal organizations may be at risk from predatory adolescent ones that have the energy but require the respectability of an older player in the market. Rates of change will be low, and neutral to negative. A negative rate of change means that the changes are likely to detract from customer satisfaction.

An organization that recognizes the menopause stage can take steps to rejuvenate itself, and this may mean hard decisions. The aim is to become vibrant again, but it must ensure that the changes it makes are the ones its customers want. Later in this chapter we shall see an organization that has been very successful at this rejuvenation: Rover cars in the UK. We have already looked at P&O, which went through major changes in the 1960s and 1970s with the declining passenger shipping market and has emerged, rejuvenated to be as good, if not better, than ever by finding out the changes its customers wanted.

The model an organization should be aiming for is shown in figure 24.

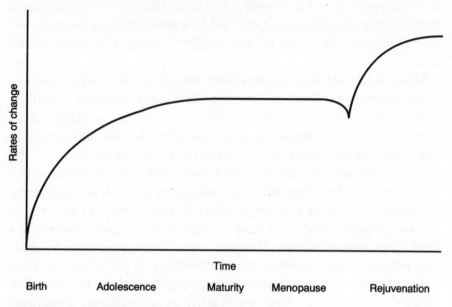

Figure 24 Organizational rejuvenation

Decline

One hopes that it doesn't happen, but where are Pan Am, the US passenger shipping industry, and many retail stores that were household names? Gone. If an organization cannot compete by making the changes customers require, it will decline and die or else be swallowed up by a more successful competitor. Rates of change will be increasingly high as restructuring upon restructuring occurs and there is a frantic attempt to deliver something that 'pays the wages', but they are often very negative, i.e. customer satisfaction decreases. These are organizations that work hard – but are working hard at losing the customer.

HOWLER

A fast food establishment, not one of the bigger chains. Lunch time and it is nearly empty.
   Customer: 'Can I have a cheese filling in my baked potato?'
   Server: 'No, it's not on the menu. Look; it's up on the wall.'
   Customer: 'Have you any cheese?'
   Server: 'Yes, but it's not for baked potatoes.'

> and so on for a few minutes. Eventually the customers says,
> 'You deserve to be empty' and walks away.
>   Server: '*%$@' (i.e. unprintable).

You could almost call this 'Positive Lethargy': it would have been easier for the customer to have been given what he wanted rather than for the server to argue with him. You normally only argue with customers once; you don't normally see them again.

The Rover Group, one of the UK's premier automobile manufacturers, had its roots in the nationalized British Leyland concern, which was a prime target for privatization by the incoming Conservative government in 1979 and was sold to British Aerospace (BAe) in 1988. That Rover has been successful in becoming a customer-orientated, high-quality manufacturer is shown by its acquisition in 1995 by the German car maker, BMW.

The Western automobile industry was decimated by Japanese expansion in the early 1980s. The total US capacity closures totalled 1 817 000 units, whereas Japanese implants into the US, i.e. Japanese companies opening up US factories, totalled 1 720 000. At this time Rover was a relatively small player in an increasingly global market-place, manufacturing 500 000 vehicles annually. The Rover name was well known and in the past Rover had been at the top end of the market with a reputation for quality products. Although the company was not actually nationalized, the Government had a major shareholding during the 1960s and 1970s. British Leyland had some mediocre products, and Rover found itself competing in the UK market not only with its traditional rivals, Ford and General Motors (branded as Vauxhall in the UK), but also with Nissan, Toyota and Honda.

One of the first changes in the rejuvenation of Rover was to link up with Honda, which, much later, acquired its own UK manufacturing base, in order to acquire insight into Japanese manufacturing and management techniques for joint projects. Thus, the Rover 200 series and the Honda Concerto were very similar products, branded differently but of equal quality. Using the product life cycle model (chapter 2), Rover was trying to capture a greater share of a saturated market. There is only one way to accomplish this, and that is to gain customers from your competitors.

Rover's senior management developed the 'Rover Vision':

Rover is internationally renowned for customer satisfaction.

To achieve the vision, Rover decided on four strategic thrusts based on an overriding product strategy of differentiation, i.e. to aim its products at the premium, niche end of each market segment. In the UK, as in other European countries and the USA, there are specific segments of the automobile market:

- Small cars
- Family cars
- Fleet buyers (business use)
- Off-road vehicles
- Luxury cars

It was Rover's intention to implement changes so that it would be offering products at the top end of each market through a family of models, all of which would offer considerable value added plus the prestige of the Rover brand. As with many other automobile manufacturers, this has resulted in numerical series: Rover 100, 200, 400, 600 and 800 series, and the famous Land Rover series, with the Land Rover Defender, the Land Rover Discovery and the Range Rover models.

The four strategic thrusts were:

- Achieve number one position on customer satisfaction index (this is an independently-published index, of great importance to the motor industry).
- Reduce break even.
- Reduce dependency on the UK market.
- Move upmarket.

In the context of this book, it is the first of these thrusts that is of most interest.

How do you become the number one for customer satisfaction in an industry that is full of high quality competitors?

The first changes need to be internal. Rover set about developing and disseminating its strategy through project groups and training. Everybody who worked for Rover needed to be aware of the issues. Indeed, charts showing progress on the strategic plan were placed in prominent positions throughout the factories, and these charts showed the name of the senior manager responsible for each area. Senior managers were putting their reputations on the line.

Rover also identified nine key business processes that would lead to being number one for customer satisfaction:

- Product improvement
- New product introduction
- Logistics
- Sales/distribution/service
- Manufacture
- Maintenance
- Business planning
- Corporate learning
- Management of people

Let us see how these impact on the customer.

The bottom line for the customer is the highest quality vehicle at the lowest possible cost and with the highest reliability and the lowest servicing costs. This is a dynamic industry, where product innovation is occurring very rapidly. In 1990 only very expensive vehicles had airbags; now they are standard. In 1970, radios and heaters were optional extras on some vehicles; it would be hard to find a car without them as standard today.

By talking to customers and offering what they wanted, Rover was able to establish (or re-establish) its position as a quality manufacturer with value added.

Rover dealers offer excellent sales and service; Rover was one of the first manufacturers to offer to take your vehicle back within 1 month or 1000 miles (1600 km), whatever the reason. Its first advertisement for this service showed an owner who found that his garage was just too short for his new Rover. Excellent finance deals, high quality design of vehicles, both functionally and cosmetically (the Rover radiator grille is quite distinctive), and excellent quality of manufacture have gone a long way towards fulfilling the vision. What is equally important is that Rover talks to its customers, both at point of sale and via questionnaires after sale, to ensure that it is delivering what the customer wants. New customers are telephoned after they have had the vehicle for a short time to find out if there are any problems.

The key change has been listening to customers and developing products that they want at a price that they deem equitable. Link this to the development of a business vision and the identification of key business processes and you have the key ingredients for excellent customer satisfaction and ongoing customer loyalty.

GOLDEN RULE

You must listen to your customers to find out what they want.

And, in such a highly competitive industry:

GOLDEN RULE

If you don't look after your customers, somebody else will.

A Rover owner had been in possession of a 200 series vehicle for 15 months when, after a period of very heavy rain, he found that the floor on the driver's side was awash. This occurred on the Monday morning of a very busy week for that particular customer. The dealer was telephoned at 8.30 a.m., and by 9.30 a.m. the vehicle was in the repair shop and a loan vehicle (an example of the newest model) had been provided and additional insurance cover arranged. At the end of the day the fault was still proving illusive; leaks are very difficult to trace and the weather conditions had been especially severe. The dealer, part of the Hartwell Group in the UK, had no hesitation; keep the loan vehicle for another day and that will allow us to ensure that the fault has been rectified.

One could argue that a vehicle should not develop a fault but, as we have seen in previous chapters, customers do experience problems. By taking ownership of this particular problem, the dealer ended up with a satisfied customer and may well have ensured a future sale. By looking at loaning a car as a form of extended test drive, there was the possibility of repeat business brought about by reflecting Rover's commitment to putting the customer at the centre of operations.

Rover is a big company but everybody can ensure that their business processes and the changes they introduce are linked to the overriding need to obtain ongoing customer satisfaction.

THINK POINT

How do changes that you or your organization have introduced both meet the needs of the organization and aid customer satisfaction?

This book has looked at a number of organizations, from the very small to the multinational. They all have one thing in common: they have all demonstrated a commitment to customer satisfaction. The next chapter looks at those who haven't – examples of where it all went wrong.

SUMMARY

This chapter has been about the management of change, from both the individual and the organizational point of view. Change may not be comfortable but it is inevitable and it needs to be managed in such a way that both the organization and the customer benefit.

8

I Can't Get No Satisfaction

A WHOLE 'PACK' OF HOWLERS

In this chapter we are going to give you more examples of Howlers, like those that have appeared throughout the book. The authors guarantee that all of these incidents actually happened. There may well be some very red faces among our readers if they recognize themselves here. However, rest assured that we will not be naming names, except to say that none of these incidents involved any of the organizations mentioned by name in this book.

HOWLER

A customer is sitting in a diner, waiting to order. He doesn't bother with the menu because he knows what he wants and it isn't on the menu but this chain of diners will usually make it up for you. He orders a toasted bacon sandwich. No problem!

When it arrives he finds that it is a toasted bacon and tomato sandwich. He hates cooked tomatoes!

'Excuse me, I ordered a bacon sandwich. You've brought me one with tomatoes in.'

'Yes, just as it says on the menu, sir, Toasted Bacon and Tomato Sandwich.'

'But I only asked for bacon! And anyway it's not on the menu.'

'Yes it is, sir, since the beginning of this week when the new menus were printed! If you only wanted bacon you should have told me to leave off the tomato!'

'But I didn't know it came with tomato. Should I also have

asked you to leave off the mushrooms . . . or the potatoes . . . or the egg? How do I know what to ask you to leave off when I only wanted bacon?'

'Perhaps you should have looked at the menu!'

HOWLER

On a flight to Singapore, about half way through the night-time, thirteen-hour flight, a woman approaches the curtained area where the cabin crew are based, to ask for a drink of orange juice. Just as she reaches the curtain, it is suddenly pulled back and a cabin attendant rushes out.

'Please, could I have an ora—'

'I haven't time to deal with *you*. You'll have to wait!'

The woman returned to her seat, furious.

In fact, what was actually happening was that in the forward cabin, someone had fainted and her husband had rushed down to tell the cabin attendant. She had stopped what she was doing immediately and was responding to the emergency when she encountered the unfortunate thirsty passenger. She carried out the necessary first aid and the patient was restored to normal.

The thirsty passenger knew nothing of this, only that a cabin attendant had been very rude to her during the flight.

So, in this case, far from a disaster being turned into a triumph, what should have been a triumph was turned into a disaster!

There are at least two hotels in the heart of England, and there may be many more, where you receive the same amount of coffee in a cafetiere for four people as you do for two, but are charged twice the amount!

HOWLER

A couple checked into a hotel and were shown up to their room. The brochure said there would be a minibar but there wasn't. The porter promised to tell the manager, who would arrange to send one to the room. It didn't arrive during the first day, so the couple mentioned it again. When they came back on the second day from an all-day excursion, it still wasn't there, so they mentioned it again.

When they arrived back at their room at the end of the third day, behold, there it was located in the corner of the room, which was just as well, because the temperature outside was approaching 100 degrees and they were both desperate for a long cool drink.

There was no key!

Two days later, they set off to catch their homeward flight without ever gaining access to the minibar!

HOWLER

A guest woke up abruptly at two o'clock in the morning. The fire alarm was ringing. His wife sat bolt upright too. He felt the adrenaline rising as he remembered that they were on the fifth floor and they would have to use the stairs. Yes, the stairs . . . now where were they?

He regretted not having taken more notice of the fire precautions on the inside of the door. Never mind, he thought, he remembered a staircase a few doors away. No time to lose, they had to move now.

They bolted for the door of their room, half expecting to find acrid smoke billowing in at them. They had, almost by reflex, covered their mouths with handkerchiefs just in case.

They opened the door onto a scene of . . . absolute serenity.

There was no smoke.

There was no shouting.

There was no panic.

There was no one else around, no movement at all!

Yet the fire alarm was still ringing.

He looked over the edge of the low wall that ran along the edge of the open corridor, so that he could look down at the central court – nothing.

It was fairly obvious by now that they weren't in any immediate danger so he went back into the room, leaving the door open and leaving his wife at the door on guard for any flames or smoke that might begin to lick up towards the fifth floor.

He rang reception.

A very polite voice answered, 'Yes, how can I help you?'

'What do you mean, how can you help me? The fire alarm's ringing.'

'Oh it often does that, don't worry about it, it's usually a false alarm. We've sent a couple of staff to look round just to check, but if I were you I'd go back to sleep.'

HOWLER

Two customers were enjoying an excellent meal in a restaurant in one of the more fashionable areas of Rome. The starter had been excellent, and the main course had been a delight. They were now reaching the stage where they wanted to dwell over the sweet menu, firstly because Italian sweets are world famous and the restaurant had a superb selection, secondly because they needed a rest between the courses before they felt they could do justice to a sweet, and thirdly they could linger over a glass of wine and spend a long time choosing.

It was about ten o'clock in the evening and the restaurant was pretty full. In fact, they had been placed on a table for four because it had been the only one available when they arrived, but there was now a table for two free to one side of them and a table for four available behind them.

The waiter arrived and they indicated that they would like more time.

The waiter, on the other hand, indicated that there was a party of eight regular customers arriving and he required this table of four to put together with the free table for four, and would the two of them please vacate their table and move over there to the table for two!

They protested loudly, but while they did so the waiter and two colleagues who had arrived as reinforcements swiftly and expertly laid the table for two and moved the customers' belongings onto it. It was such a slick operation that it was clearly not the first time it had been executed!

The customers forgot about their sweet and complained profusely. But no one was listening because all attention had now focused on the incoming party of eight.

The two paid up and left, but no one really noticed them leave.

HOWLER

A businessman arrived at his hotel after a long drive. It was after eleven o'clock in the evening. He dialled room service and ordered a steak sandwich. He was promised that it would arrive in some twenty minutes.

He was stiff and tired after the long drive and he really wanted a bath. However, he didn't have time to enjoy one before room service arrived so thought he would unpack, have a drink from the fridge and the meal would arrive, after which he would watch a little bit of television while the meal went down and then have a bath.

After half an hour he rang room service to check where his meal was.

They had never heard of him or his meal!

However, they would send it up straight away, in about fifteen minutes.

'I could have had my bath,' he muttered under his breath.

The meal arrived at about half an hour after midnight.

He looked down at a plate of steak sandwich and chips; they had not even left him any salt to put on them!

He rang room service, who brought him some salt.

At 12.40 he sat down to eat . . . and he still hadn't taken his bath! And the meal was horrible: 'And I bet the bed's too hard!'

HOWLER

A customer took his trolley around the supermarket then joined the queue at the check-out. He managed to queue, be served, load up his purchases, pay and leave without once ever being even looked at by the check-out assistant, who was talking to the supervisor at the time.

HOWLER

A family eagerly awaited their meal to be delivered to their home, a service offered by a local take-away restaurant. It was early evening.

Most of the meal appeared to have been deep fried a second time and was generally inedible. They didn't bother to complain, but not only do they not use that particular restaurant again, they have never used similar services offered by other nearby restaurants.

HOWLER

A guest unpacked his suitcase in a hotel room and changed, ready to go to dinner. He freshened up and used the loo. He went to flush the toilet but there was no flush handle!

He looked at the top of the cistern for a button to push, which is the usual alternative. No button!

He looked on the floor to see if there was a treadle to stand upon as there is in railway carriages. There was none!

He walked away from the toilet in case it was one of those that flush automatically when you leave. It wasn't.

He walked back to it in case it was one that flushed automatically as you approach. It wasn't.

Amid growing panic, he looked around the walls to see if there were any other buttons or handles. There weren't any. The only thing on the wall was the toilet roll holder.

He turned his attention to the pipes running into the cistern. There were quite a few nuts and screws holding the various bits together. Blood pressure rising, he felt each one just to see if it was some kind of concealed flush. Predictably, none of them was.

He looked around the room again and gave the matter some serious thought. He eyed up every handle, even that on the bathroom door, in case it, incredibly, had any link with the toilet. Of course, it hadn't.

There was nothing for it but to ring reception. The young lady was very polite but all the same was incredulous, 'What, no handle at all? We've been using that room quite normally and no one else has had any trouble. There's got to be a handle or something.'

'Yes, that's what I thought, I can't believe it either, but I've looked everywhere.'

'I'd better come up.'

'OK', replied a by this time very embarrassed guest.

In a very few minutes the receptionist arrived and the guest let her into the room rather sheepishly. He certainly couldn't look her in the eye.

She went into the bathroom and looked around for a few moments and at first she couldn't find anything either.

Then, the guest, who was sitting in a chair in the main room, heard the toilet flush. He couldn't believe it. He felt a mixture of one part relief and three parts embarrassment.

What had happened was that the toilet roll holder had been removed or fallen off and never replaced. The toilet roll was in fact on the flush handle so when he had used it he had actually touched the handle!

So near and yet so far!

He hasn't had the courage to face up to the receptionist again, despite the fact that she really dealt with the situation very tactfully and was very apologetic, so he now uses a different hotel in the same town.

HOWLER

The driver pulled the coach up outside the hotel where several groups of holiday-makers were sitting in anticipation, waiting for him to arrive. They were generally excited as this excursion was going to take them through some very scenic areas of Oahu, the principal island of the Hawaiian chain.

Their final destination was Waimea Park, which is famous for its high divers and outstanding natural beauty.

The passengers made themselves comfortable and the driver introduced himself.

He began by telling them a little about Honolulu, the capital, and about Waikiki Beach, the famous resort area.

He then went on to tell them about every point of interest, or lack of it, *en route*. Once they drove through a very scenic area where there were few landmarks, so he went on to tell them about his family, and then about himself. In fact he went on . . . and on . . . and on.

By the time they arrived at Waimea, many of the passengers were in a mutinous state. There were discussions concerning sharing taxis for the journey back.

Having enjoyed the four-hour stay at the park, the passengers gingerly returned to the bus, steeling themselves for another onslaught on their eardrums.

'Perhaps it won't be so bad going back. We must have just about heard everything now. Surely he can't have much more to say.'

They were proved wrong almost immediately as they encountered a five-mile tailback of vehicles all intending to leave the area at the same time. The driver had no difficulty whatsoever in filling in for the duration of this minor set-back with details of his life as a young boy. So, having moved about seven miles in three quarters of an hour, the passengers were by now completely up to date with his life history up to the point where he joined the excursion company.

It was a long journey home.

HOWLER

A couple are staying in a small hotel in France. They are only staying for one night as they are on their way south. The hotel is very pleasant with attractive rooms and is family run. However, it doesn't have a restaurant.

This is not a problem as there are several interesting places to eat within a five-minute walk, so the guests go off to find one.

They have a lovely meal and return at about nine o'clock.

To their horror, the hotel is completely in darkness and the front door is locked. They have their room keys but no outside door keys.

Their first reaction is that they have somehow lost track of time and that it must in fact be around midnight. They look over at the village clock tower, which is illuminated, and are reassured by the fact that it shows five past nine.

There is no other option than to ring the doorbell and hope that someone hears it.

There is no doorbell!

The only way they can attract attention is to bang on the big glass window which forms the entire front of the hotel.

After several minutes, the proprietor appears in a white night smock and Rip Van Winkle hat.

The proprietor has clearly been awoken from a deep sleep, probably of a hundred minutes rather than a hundred years, and is equally clearly not amused.

'Le clef, le clef [the key, the key],' he shouted, pointing behind them.

'Yes, we know, we haven't got one,' the lady responded in reasonable French.

The proprietor let them in with abundant bad grace. He pointed once again behind him, where there was a key rack with a hook for each room. Not a single key was hanging on the rack.

Light was now beginning to dawn in the minds of the holiday-makers. It turned out that guests are reminded in a notice near the door to hang up their keys on the appropriate numbered hook whenever they go out of the hotel.

When the proprietor sees that all of the keys have gone, he assumes that all of the guests have retired to bed. If not, their room key would be hanging there. The alternative possibility that a guest may have forgotten to hang the key there when they went out was not considered. Tonight he had fancied an early night and there were no room keys, so he had closed the hotel and retired for the night – until he was so rudely awoken, by inconsiderate guests who don't even bother to read instructions.

HOWLER

In a British hotel, breakfast was available from seven o'clock – not five to seven, but from exactly seven o'clock. It was a self-service breakfast but the beverages were ordered from the waiter and were brought to the table.

The guest was attending a course at the hotel and was part of a bigger group. Although he was alone and it had only just turned seven o'clock, the waiter insisted that he sit on the large table for ten people that had been set up for the company.

He ordered some coffee. He was invited to go and help himself to the Full English Breakfast, which was set up in large tureens on a central table.

He decided to wait until his coffee arrived. There was no point in trying to eat anything until he had his first cup of the day.

By ten past seven it had still not arrived.

'Yes it's just on its way sir.'

He thought he would fill in the time by going up to select his breakfast from what was a really good selection. He returned to his seat with an excellent breakfast – but there was still no coffee.

He pressed on with the breakfast because he didn't want it to go cold. He was just reaching the last slice of bacon when his coffee arrived.

A really good breakfast, he thought, pity about the coffee, pity about the service. If only the coffee had been self-service too!

A conversation on an *inter-island* flight before takeoff went something like this:

'Excuse me, miss, I don't seem to have a life jacket under my seat.'

'That's all right, madam, don't worry, this flight doesn't fly over water.'

HOWLER

A letter of complaint was sent to a well-known airline outlining the fact that there had been a delay of over an hour, that no one had explained what had caused it or how long the delay would last and that there had been no cabin crew to be seen throughout the whole period of the delay.

The complainant received a reply from headquarters indicating that the cabin crew were always available, and more or less suggesting that he hadn't looked hard enough.

He responded with an ironic apology, indicating that, of course, the customer services manager had a far better view of the cabin from his office at headquarters than he, the customer, had sitting on the plane!

References

Adams, J.L., Hayes, J. and Hopson, B. (1976), *Transitions – Understanding Managing Personal Change*. Oxford, Martin Robertson.

Cartwright, R., Collins, M., Green, G. and Candy, A. (1993), *Managing People*. Oxford, Blackwell.

Cartwright, R., Collins, M., Green, G. and Candy, A. (1993), *Managing Operations*. Oxford, Blackwell.

Cartwright, R., Collins, M., Green, G. and Candy, A. (1993), *Managing Finance and Information*. Oxford, Blackwell.

Cartwright, R., Collins, M., Green, G. and Candy, A. (1996), *In Charge of Yourself*. Oxford, Blackwell .

Dawkins, R. (1976), *The Selfish Gene*. Oxford, Oxford University Press.

Eddy, P., Potter, E. and Page, B. (1976), *Destination Disaster*. London, Hart-Davies.

Gregory, M. (1994), *Dirty Tricks – British Airways' Secret War against Virgin Atlantic*. London, Little, Brown & Co.

Goyal, N. (1995), Quoted in *Jetwings*, 1(1), March 1995, Singapore. Sparhawk PTE Ltd.

Harris, T.A. (1970), *I'm OK – You're OK*. London, Pan.

Irving, C. (1993), *Wide Body, The Making of the Boeing 747*. London, Hodder & Stoughton.

Johnson, G. and Scholes, K. (1984), *Exploring Corporate Strategy*. London, Prentice Hall.

Klundas, A., (1992), *Great Passenger Ships of the World Today*. Sparkford, Patrick Stephens.

Kotler, P. (1980), *Marketing Management*, 4th edn. New York, Prentice Hall.

Lewin, K. (1951), *Field Theory in Social Science*, ed. Dowin-Cartwright. New York, Harper.

Maslow, A. (1970), *Motivation and Personality*. New York, Harper & Row.

Ohmae, K. (1982), *The Mind of the Strategists*. New York, McGraw-Hill.

Peters, T. (1987), *Thriving on Chaos*. New York, Alfred A. Knopf Inc.

Peters, T. and Waterman, R. (1982), *In Search of Excellence*. New York, Harper & Row.

Porter, M.E. (1980), *Competitive Strategy*. New York, Free Press.

Porter, M.E. (1985), *Competitive Advantage*. New York, Free Press.

Stoppard, M. (1980), *Miriam Stoppard's Healthcare*. London, Weidenfeld & Nicolson.

Tice, L. (1989), *Investment in Excellence* (multimedia). Seattle, Pacific Institute.

Ward, D. (1994), *The Berlitz Complete Guide to Cruising and Cruise Ships 1994*. Oxford, Berlitz.

Wille, E. (1992), *Quality: Achieving Excellence*. London, Century Business (*Sunday Times* Business Skills series).

Index